VET CENTER
1600 Halsted
Chicago Heights, IL 60411
(312) 754-0340

VIETNAM: THE BATTLE COMES HOME

VET CENTER
1600 Halsted
Chicago Heights, IL 60411
(312) 754-0340

VIETNAM: THE BATTLE COMES HOME

A Photographic Record of Post-Traumatic Stress With Selected Essays

Photographs by Gordon Baer
Edited by Nancy Howell-Koehler

Morgan & Morgan

1984

Acknowledgment

I want to thank the greatest contributor of all—the Vietnam vet who continuously—even during unbelievable moments of grief and anguish echoed the message—"if helping you produce this story will prevent another vet going through what I am—tell me what I can do." G.B.

© Copyright 1984 by Gordon Baer

All rights reserved in all countries. No part of this book may be reproduced or translated in any form whatsoever without permission in writing from the publisher.

Published by Morgan & Morgan, Inc.
145 Palisade Street
Dobbs Ferry, New York 10522

International Standard Book Number 0-87100-199-3
Library of Congress Catalog Card Number 84-61115

Printed in U.S.A. by Morgan Press, Dobbs Ferry, New York.
Cover and Book Design by Julius Freedman

To Perry

Preface
Evolution of the Photographic Series

My first thoughts concerning Vietnam occurred while I attended college at the University of Louisville—and—my feelings were that it was a place to be avoided at all costs. I had little more knowledge of Vietnam, or the people who fought there until one day eighteen years later when I crossed the hall from my office to the Cincinnati Vet Center to compare rents.

The stories the counselors told me were fascinating. It sounded like they were shaman producing unique, magic and often successful cures for an illness that had to that time, not even been named; a malady that attacked like a seething swarm affecting people in many ways—all of them fraught with misery.

My own actions after my visit to a group therapy session were indeed different. I sat at a restaurant writing...rather than eating. I was recording my feelings of the previous two hours, feelings that resulted in a major question: "Why did men who fought so hard to survive in Vietnam come home wishing only to die?" It was clear that 'men who had thought they had finished with the war discovered the war wasn't finished with them'. I felt the need to make others aware of what I had heard that night and decided, if they would allow me—to *show* what the vets were saying.

Although my enthusiasm for this project was apparently readily received by the vets, I wasn't able to get into the private lives of these men and their families until one morning when I stopped by the Vet Center to talk to counselor, Bernie Evans. I was told Bernie was out looking for a missing vet, Bob Watson, who it was later discovered had left a suicide note in his car found by the river. My manner of photographing the search and subsequent friendship with the Watson family suddenly brought me close to the personal lives of many vets—lives that I heard about at the Vet Center, but required my *being there* to share and to show.

Initially I had planned to attempt writing the story as well as photographing it. Then I realized I was getting in over my head and I called a good friend and freelance writer, Leslie Major, and asked if she would be interested in joining me on the story. The help that she gave me was invaluable.

Vets began to involve us in their family crises as well as calling us the night before an Agent Orange test or a job interview, so that we could understand and participate in their day-to-day frustrations.

My hope was, and is, that these photographs and text might begin to answer the questions that initially came to my mind and that continue to be asked by an increasingly receptive public to enable us by our questions and actions to heal ourselves of the Vietnam experience.

—*Gordon Baer*

Contents

Chapter I	An Introduction to Post-Traumatic Stress Disorder:	10
	Carl Trocki, Ph.D.	
	Robert J. Lifton, M.D.	
	John P. Wilson, Ph.D.	
	Jim Goodwin, Psy.D.	
	Tom Keller and Jerry Atchison	
	Arthur S. Blank, Jr., M.D.	
	Arthur Egendorf, Ph.D.	
	Peter Marin	
	Robert O. Muller	
Chapter II	Living in the Past	50
Chapter III	Families in Transition	66
Chapter IV	Facing the Problems	76
Chapter V	The Price	92

Outreach Program Directory
Bibliography and References

Ten years and no relief.

Chapter I

An Introduction to Post-Traumatic Stress Disorder

Essays by:

Carl Trocki, Ph.D.
Robert J. Lifton, M.D.
John P. Wilson, Ph.D.
Jim Goodwin, Psy.D.
Tom Keller and Jerry Atchison
Arthur S. Blank Jr., M.D.
Arthur Egendorf, Ph.D.
Peter Marin
Robert O. Muller

Why Remind Ourselves of the Vietnam War?
Carl A. Trocki, Ph.D.

The function of the historian in society is to "remember." This is particularly true when the past is one filled with pain, when remembering brings only bitterness. Such has been the Vietnam experience.

This is why it is crucial to study the Vietnam War, and to understand its causes, effects and the soldiers who fought there. The veterans are the human part of this story...they are among the "scar tissue" of our society. Because the war itself was the wound, we now must sit down and listen to veterans tell their stories and help them deal with their own consciences. We need to learn what they did, what they were forced to do, and what they have had to endure since the war.

If we are to grow in wisdom, it is important that the "lessons" of Vietnam be understood. Not only must we understand the mistakes, so that we do not repeat them, but also, we have to know what we did that was right. We have all suffered from the impact of this war as individuals as well as a nation. The issues of the Vietnam War are far too important to be left to the pronouncements of our leaders. In a democratic society, all the people share the responsibility for creating their own history.

Carl A. Trocki, PhD, is an Associate Professor of History at Thomas More College in Covington, Kentucky. He specializes in Southeast Asian History and has written extensively on the recent history and politics of the region. He spent nearly eight years living and working in various parts of Southeast Asia during the Vietnam War.

An upside down flag symbolizes distress.

Home from the War ("Epilogue")
Robert J. Lifton, M.D.

Is the war over? A cease-fire agreement has been signed (January 1973), and the President has proclaimed "Peace with Honor." Shortly before the cease-fire, American B-52s carried out their "Christmas bombing" of Hanoi and Haiphong, two weeks of indiscriminate high-altitude "carpet bombing" employing the greatest amount of destructive power in the history of aerial warfare. Most of the world responded with strong condemnation. There was no mass protest in the United States, though there were many expressions of outrage and a compelling national campaign was mounted to raise money to rebuild Bach Mai Hospital in Hanoi. The American reaction to the cease-fire was even more equivocal, probably best characterized as joyless relief.

A few days after the announcement of the cease-fire, I met in New Haven with a group of antiwar veterans, some of whom I knew well from personal talks and rap groups. We had planned to get together a week later, but one of them telephoned to suggest that we meet right away because "the guys were having pretty strong reactions." As soon as we sat down they made it clear that the essence of those reactions was rage.

One veteran described how, right after the announcement, he found himself losing control. He broke a window in his room and drove off in his car at breakneck speed with a half-conscious intent to "smash into something"—until he was able to restrain himself and examine what he was doing and feeling. That night he had two dreams, both mostly reenactments of actual events in Vietnam: one of the men in his unit shooting Vietnamese civilians—"men, women, children, everyone"; the other of a buddy "hit by a rocket, his guts falling out...trying to hold them in...even though he was dead." The other men expressed similar combinations of reactivated memories and immediate rage, and emphasized that "what especially makes us gag is talk about peace with honor."

In softer tones another veteran said, "There is no sense of an ending. Usually war—or anything—is supposed to have a beginning, a middle, and an end...This is a false ending." He spoke of "the incredible reluctance of the country to face what did go on there," and another added that "a real ending to this war would be that America would have to come to terms with what the war has been all along."

The men went on to speak of the tendency of Americans to be more preoccupied with the return of prisoners of war than with the larger questions of war and peace. "They need heroes" was the way one put it. We talked of the desperate effort to salvage something ennobling from a degrading war—to focus on the courage and strength of men subjected to prolonged incarceration by the enemy, or on that of their wives or parents in waiting for them. The veterans had conflicted feelings about the whole matter—a mixture of sympathy for the returning POWs, whom they viewed as war victims much like themselves, along with resentment of the government's manipulation of national feelings about POWs in ways that distracted Americans from the war's truths. As one man said, somewhat uneasily, "I'm withholding emotion from them."

A few had made an attempt at celebration. "We thought, Well, it's over now. That's what we've been struggling for. Why not have a few drinks together?" But when they got to the bar, they found their hearts were not in it and left early: "We made believe we should celebrate—but it just didn't work." They noted that most other veterans they knew, including those who took no stand on the war, were also "on downs"—in low moods if not actually depressed.

An added influence on the veterans' responses was the death of former President Lyndon Johnson just before the cease-fire was signed. "We had to realize that it wasn't just him—it was the whole country—and then there was nowhere to place the rage." That rage became more diffuse, so that one of the most militant of the men could say, "I'll always be at war while

I'm in this country—it's the only way to survive."

Again and again the men returned to the phrase, "Peace with Honor." They pointed out that America was still at war in Laos and Cambodia; that America had a lot to do with the fighting still going on in Vietnam; that we were leaving behind various kinds of agents to engage in covert warfare throughout Indochina, and maintaining a tremendous financial and technological presence in South Vietnam. They spoke bitterly of news reports of "the last American to die in Vietnam" and then of "the first American to die after the cease-fire," which sounded to them both "like a baseball score" and "a new body count." What they were saying was that the counterfeit universe of the war had been extended into the cease-fire and beyond. Hence one man concluded: "It isn't peace. And there's no honor."

Yet they knew something had changed. Above all, their own status was suddenly different. "We are no longer dissidents against the war but just hippies" was the way one man put it. As veteran-dissidents they had standing and credibility, but as troublesome hippies they would have neither. In other words they perceived the cease-fire, in the form it took, as a negotiated interruption of war-making precluding confrontation of the war—as an officially-sponsored termination of their own special survivor mission as antiwar veterans. Their rage as well as their painful inner reenactment of the war had to do with their sense of being again rebuffed, this time definitively, and left to stew in their own conflicts. Their government had, as one man said, "once and for all closed the door"—shut out the truth, the possibility of illumination and of new beginning. Hence the additional reaction he experienced to the cease-fire: "Was this it? Was this all?"

Yet that door could not be locked, not even fully closed. Even before the cease-fire many veterans had been thinking about and beginning to act upon the next stage of their survivor mission. Over the years they have been bringing truths about the war into many corners of American life. A number of them have been focusing on the issue of amnesty, which they sense to be inseparable from their own mission. And the six or seven of us who met in New Haven formed a new rap group for the dual purpose of exploring changing personal emotions and considering possible ethical and political directions for the immediate future—precisely the concerns of many rap groups that continue to take shape among Vietnam veterans.

Some veterans, ambivalent about having the term "post-Vietnam syndrome" applied to themselves, suggest that it is more genuinely applicable to America at large. The psychological truth of that claim lies in the combination of a cease-fire that is not quite a peace, and the powerful war-linked residuum in the American people of confusion, guilt, rage, and betrayal. We have become a nation of troubled survivors of a war not yet over and still just distantly perceived. We experience a continuing sense of threat, of "immersion in death," and the resulting survivor conflicts can take many forms. We have already seen the beginnings of the most pernicious kind of survivor formulation on the part of government spokesmen: one which attributes the prolonging of the war, and by inference the suffering of everyone, to war opponents and protesters. That formulation combines scapegoating with still more ominous currents of potential victimization.

But there are more hopeful directions of survivor formulation in which error and wrongdoing can be acknowledged and the death-and-rebirth imagery of survival called forth. In that spirit, the sister of America's longest-held prisoner of war, a man known to be a leader of POW "hawks," tells us that when her brother comes back he will have much to learn about the social change that has occurred in this country in his absence. "In 1964, when my brother was shot down, there was complete faith in the government, the government knew best. The military and the uniform were looked upon with a tremendous amount of respect. All that has changed considerably." Originally in agreement with him about all this, she has since joined the antiwar and chicano movements: "The mentality that calls Vietnamese 'gooks' is the same mentality that calls brown people 'spics.' It's the same battle." The pain and suffering surrounding the Vietnam War have made available to virtually everyone at least the possibility of illumination and growth—if one can permit oneself to feel and take some responsibility toward that pain and suffering.

As for me, I think I have learned a great deal. But like many others, I remain dissatisfied both with what I know and with what I can do with that knowledge. In pursuing the dialectic of "resistance and contemplation" so eloquently lived out by James Douglass, I have, together with others in the arts and professions, engaged in two acts of modest civil disobedience to protest the war. We were trying to express our own 'Nuremberg obligation,' according to the principle laid down by American international legal authorities after World War II at Nuremberg that citizens had the responsibility to resist war crimes of their own government. Originally stated as applicable to everyone, that principle has so far been applied only by victors to those they have defeated. The Indochina War, with its combination of massive American illegality and criminality, and its multiple confusions concerning victors and vanquished, would seem to be an ideal war around which to revive a more universal Nuremberg obligation.

That obligation takes one immediately to such issues as the implementation of the cease-fire accords, the sustained American intervention in Indochina and its potential for covert warfare, and, perhaps most centrally, that of unconditional amnesty for resisters, exiles and deserters.

Now Vietnam veterans are everywhere. They are an embarrassment to the country in the unanswerable questions raised by their very presence. I meet increasing numbers of them at campuses I visit in various parts of the United States. They speak with mixtures of anxiety and wisdom of their future and the country's, and of the kinds of American leadership that might emerge from the Vietnam war experience. We talk of survivor imagery in leaders being twenty years behind the times, so that the men who insisted upon "standing fast" and "staying the course" in Vietnam were filtering the situation through retained images of 'Munich' and of the disastrous results of Western European "appeasement" of Hitler in 1938. The veterans raise hard questions about whether survivor imagery from the Vietnam War will in turn be inappropriately misleading for a crisis twenty years from now. All of which suggests that wisdom does not come easily, and also that we may just have learned something from Vietnam.

The veterans I talked to sense the fragility of their own insight, psychological or political. They know themselves all too capable of embracing idols and taking wrong turnings. Looking about they see many of their veteran "brothers" overwhelmed with bitterness or on drugs, in one way or another immobilized. They themselves experience pain that will not go away, which one of them spoke of as "an emotional devil inside of us—all of us." Like Guy Sajer, the Alsatian veteran of the German Army in World War II, they sense that "something hideous...entered our spirits to remain and haunt us forever."

I have two final images One is of the chilling contrast between peace celebrations of 1945 and 1973, as flashed on the television screen: the night of V-E Day in Times Square, film clips of pure mass joy, which I know to be authentic as I was there in that crowd, a happy nineteen-year-old medical student; and Times Square after the 1973 cease-fire—the area itself now looking seedy, almost deserted, a few Vietnam veterans gathered in anger, some drinking, others apparently on drugs, most simply enraged, screaming at the camera, at the society, about having been deceived by the war and ignored upon coming back, one specially enraged black veteran shouting, "You can tell that bastard the war isn't over."

The other image was from the meeting with Vietnam veterans described above shortly after the cease-fire. We talked about whether or not one still goes on being an antiwar veteran. One of the men spoke simultaneously of continuing war abroad and his own inner struggles, and then said firmly, and not only for himself, "I'm going to be a Vietnam veteran against the war for the rest of my life."

Reprinted from *Home From The War* by Robert J. Lifton. ©1984 by Robert J. Lifton. Reprinted by permission of Basic Books, Inc. Publishers.

Robert Jay Lifton, M.D. holds the Foundations' Fund Chair for Research in Psychiatry at Yale University. He is the author of *Death in Life: Survivors of Hiroshima*, which won the 1969 National Book Award in the sciences. In addition to *Home from the War: Vietnam Veterans—Neither Victims Nor Executioners*, Lifton has authored other books dealing with questions of war, mortality and the trauma of survival.

Two Old Veterans. While Americans fought for Vietnamese soil an honored veteran from another war displays his medals with pride, 1970.

The Process of Re-entry: Maximizing the Negative Effects of Stressors Encountered in Vietnam

John P. Wilson, Ph.D.

If you were daemonic and powerful enough to want to make someone "crazy" following a war—like Vietnam—how would you do it? If you wanted to maximize the negative effects of the stressors encountered in the line of duty in the war zone how would you do it? What would be the worst set of social, economic, political and psychological conditions you could create for the returnee?

First, you would send a young man fresh out of high school to an unpopular, controversial guerrilla war far away from home. In that war you would expose him to a high level of intensely stressful events, some so horrible and painful that it would be impossible to really talk about them later to anyone else except fellow "survivors." However, to insure maximal stress you would create a one-year tour of duty during which the combatant flies to and from the war zone, singly, *without* a cohesive, intact and emotionally supportive unit with high morale. You would also create the one-year rotation to instill a "survivor mentality" which would under-cut the process of ideological commitment to winning the war and seeing it as a noble and just cause. Then, at DEROS, you would rapidly remove the combatant from his foxhole and *singly* return him to his front porch *without* an opportunity to sort out the meaning of the experience with the men in *his* unit. Rather you would try to outprocess him into civilian status as quickly as possible. No decompression. No deprogramming. No readjustment counseling. No homecoming welcome or victory parades. Further, if you were daemonic enough you would make sure that the veteran becomes stigmatized and portrayed to the public as a "drug-crazed psychopathic killer" with no morals or impulse control over aggressive feelings. Then, too, by virtue of the selective service system the 21 or 22 year old veteran would be unable to easily re-enter the mainstream of society because he is undereducated and lacks marketable job skills. Thus, after the war he has to struggle to establish his personal identity and to find a niche in society. Further, since the war itself was so difficult you would want to make sure that there were no supportive systems in society for him, especially among mental health professionals at VA hospitals who typically find his nightmares and residual war-related anxieties unintelligible. Finally, you would want to establish a GI Bill with inadequate benefits to pay for education and job training coupled with an economy of high inflation and unemployment. Last but not least, you would want him to *feel* isolated, stigmatized, unappreciated and exploited for volunteering to serve his country. If, then, you were to do all of these things you would surely *maximize the effects of war related stresses* and insure their prolonged deleterious effects in his life. Tragically, of course, the scenario depicted above was not fictictious; rather it was the usual homecoming for most Vietnam veterans.

Reprint from Section IV, "Toward An Understanding of Post-Traumatic Stress Disorders Among Vietnam Veterans," A Testimony Before U.S. Senate Subcommittee on Veteran Affairs, May 21, 1980, Washington, D.C. by Dr. John P. Wilson. Reprinted by permission of John P. Wilson.

John P. Wilson, Ph.D. is founder and director of the Forgotten Warrior Project, funded by the Disabled American Veterans to investigate the post-military adjustment of Vietnam veterans. As a result of his research, the DAV, under Dr. Wilson's guidance, established an outreach program in over 60 cities across the nation to provide readjustment counseling. He won the Consortium on Veteran Studies' Research Award for this work. Wilson is a professor of Psychology at Cleveland State University where his current research focuses on the nature, dynamics and predictors of post-traumatic stress syndrome.

The Etiology of Combat Related Post-Traumatic Stress Disorders
Jim Goodwin, Psy.D.

The Evolution of Post-Traumatic Stress Disorder

It was not until World War I that specific clinical syndromes came to be associated with combat duty. In prior wars, it was assumed that such casualties were merely manifestations of poor discipline and cowardice. However, with the protracted artillery barrages commonplace during "The Great War," the concept evolved that the high air pressure of the exploding shells caused actual physiological damage, precipitating the numerous symptoms that were subsequently labeled "shell shock." By the end of the war, further evolution accounted for the syndrome being labeled a "war neurosis" (Glass, 1969).

During the early years of World War II, psychiatric casualties had increased some 300 percent when compared with World War I, even though the preinduction psychiatric rejection rate was three to four times higher than World War I (Figley, 1978). At one point in the war, the number of men being discharged from the service for psychiatric reasons exceeded the total number of men being newly drafted (Tiffany and Allerton, 1967).

During the Korean War, the approach to combat stress became even more pragmatic. Due to the work of Albert Glass (1954), individual breakdowns in combat effectiveness were dealt with in a very situational manner. Clinicians provided immediate onsite treatment to affected individuals, always with the expectation that the combatant would return to duty as soon as possible. The results were gratifying. During World War II, 23 percent of the evacuations were for psychiatric reasons. But in Korea, psychiatric evacuations dropped to only six percent (Bourne, 1970). It finally became clear that the situational stresses of the combatant were the primary factors leading to a psychological casualty.

Surprisingly, with American involvement in the Vietnam War, psychological battlefield casualties evolved in a new direction. What was expected from past war experiences—and what was prepared for—did not materialize. Battlefield psychological breakdown was at an all-time low, 12 per one thousand (Bourne, 1970). It was decided that use of preventive measures learned in Korea and some added situational manipulation which will be discussed later had solved the age-old problem of psychological breakdown in combat.

"My Daddy Calls Me a Vet". Veterans Day parade, 1980.

As the war continued for a number of years, some interesting additional trends were noted. Although the behavior of some combatants in Vietnam undermined fighting efficiency, the symptoms presented rarely resembled the previous classical picture of combat fatigue. As the war progressed, a previously obscure but very well documented phenomenon of World War II began to be reobserved. After the end of World War II, some men suffering from acute combat reaction, as well as some of their peers with no such symptoms at war's end, began to complain of common symptoms. These included intense anxiety, battle dreams, depression, explosive aggressive behavior and problems with interpersonal relationships, to name a few. These were found in a five-year follow-up (Futterman and Pumpian-Mindlin, 1951) and in a 20-year follow-up (Archibald and Tuddenham, 1965).

A similar trend was once more observed in Vietnam veterans as the war wore on. Both those who experienced acute combat reaction and many who did not began to complain of the above symptoms long after their combatant role had ceased. What was so unusual was the large numbers of veterans being affected after Vietnam. The pattern of neuropsychiatric disorder for combatants of World War II and Korea was quite different than for Vietnam. For both World War II and the Korean War, the incidence of neuropsychiatric disorder among combatants increased as the intensity of the wars increased. As these wars wore down, there was a corresponding decrease in these disorders until the incidence closely resembled the particular prewar periods. The prolonged or delayed symptoms noticed during the postwar periods were noted to be somewhat obscure and few in numbers; therefore, no great significance was attached to them. However, the Vietnam experience proved different. As the war in Vietnam progressed in intensity, there was no corresponding increase in neuropsychiatric casualties among combatants. It was not until the early 1970's, when the war was winding down, that neuropsychiatric disorders began to increase. With the end of direct American troop involvement in Vietnam in 1973, the number of veterans presenting neuropsychiatric disorders began to increase tremendously (President's Commission on Mental Health, 1978).

During the same period in the 1970's, many other people were experiencing varying traumatic episodes other than combat. There were large numbers of plane crashes, natural disasters, fires, acts of terrorism on civilian populations and other catastrophic events. The picture presented to many mental health professionals working with victims of these events, helping them adjust after traumatic experiences, was quite similar to the phenomenon of the troubled Vietnam veteran. The symptoms were almost identical. Finally, after much research (Figley, 1978) by various veterans' task forces and recommendations by those involved in treatment of civilian post-trauma clients, the DSM III (1980) was published with a new category; post-traumatic stress disorder, acute, chronic and/or delayed.

How the Vietnam Experience Differed from Previous Wars and Subsequently Predisposed the Combatant to the Post-Traumatic Stress Disorder: Delayed and/or Chronic Type

Remembering "The Big One".
Veterans Day parade, 1980.

When direct American troop involvement in Vietnam became a reality, military planners looked to previous war experience to help alleviate the problem of psychological disorder in combat. By then it was an understood fact that those combatants with the most combat exposure suffered the highest incidence of breakdown. In Korea this knowledge resulted in use, to some extent, of a "point system." After accumulating so many points, an individual was rotated home, regardless of the progress of the war. This was further refined in Vietnam, the outcome being the DEROS (date of expected return from overseas) system. Every individual serving in Vietnam, except general officers, knew before leaving the United States when he or she was scheduled to return. The tour lasted 12 months for everyone except the Marines who, known for their one-upmanship, did a 13-month tour. DEROS promised the combatant a way out of the war other than as a physical or psychological casualty (Kormos, 1978).

The advantages were clear: there would not be an endless period of protracted combat with the prospect of becoming a psychological casualty as the only hope for return to the United States without wounds. Rather, if a combatant could just hold together for the 12 or 13 months, he would be rotated to the United States; and, once home, he would leave the war far behind.

The disadvantages to DEROS were not as clear, and some time elapsed before they were noticed. DEROS was a very personal thing; each individual was rotated on his own with his own specific date. This meant that tours in Vietnam were solitary, individual episodes. It was rare, after the first few years of the war, that whole units were sent to the war zone simultaneously. Bourne said it best: "The war becomes a highly individualized and encapsulated event for each man. His war begins the day he arrives in the country, and ends the day he leaves" (p. 12, 1970). Bourne further states, "He feels no continuity with those who precede or follow him: He even feels apart from those who are with him but rotating on a different schedule'' (p. 42, 1970).

Because of this very individual aspect of the war, unit morale, unit cohesion and unit identification suffered tremendously (Kormos, 1978). Many studies from past wars (Grinker and Spiegel, 1945) point to the concept of how unit integrity acts as a buffer for the individual against the overwhelming stresses of combat. Many of the veterans of World War II spent weeks or months with their units returning on ships from all over the world. During the long trip home, these men and the closeness and emotional support of one another to rework the especially traumatic episodes they had experienced together. The epitaph for the Vietnam veteran, however, was a solitary plane ride home with complete strangers and a head full of grief, conflict, confusion and joy.

For every Vietnam combatant, the DEROS date became a fantasy that on a specific day all problems would cease as he flew swiftly back to the United States. The combatants believed that neither they as individuals nor the United States as a society had changed in their absence. Hundreds of thousands of men lived this fantasy from day to day. The universal popularity of short-timer calendars is evidence of this. A short-timer was a GI who was finishing his tour overseas. The calendars intricately marked off the days remaining of his overseas tour in all manner of designs with 365 spaces to fill in to complete the final design and mark that final day. The GIs overtly displayed these calendars to one another. Those with the shortest time left in the country were praised by others and would lead their peers on a fantasy excursion of how wonderful and carefree life would be as soon as they returned home. For many, this became an almost daily ritual. For those who may have ben struggling with a psychological breakdown due to the stresses of combat, the DEROS fantasy served as a major prophylactic to actual overt symptoms of acute combat reaction. For these veterans, it was a hard-fought struggle to hold on until their time came due.

The vast majority of veterans did hold on as evidenced by the low neuropsychiatric casualty rates during the war (The President's Commission on Mental Health, 1978). Rates of acute combat reaction or acute post-traumatic stress disorder were significantly lowered relative to the two previous wars. As a result, many combatants, who in previous wars might have become psychological statistics, held on somewhat tenuously until the end of their tours in Vietnam.

The struggle for most was an uphill battle. Those motivators that kept the combatant fighting—unit *esprit de corps*, small group solidarity and an ideological belief that this was the good fight (Moskos, 1975)—were not present in Vietnam. Unit *esprit* was effectively slashed by the DEROS system. Complete strangers, often GIs who were strangers even to a specific unit's specialty, were transferred into units whenever individual rotations were completed. Veterans who had finally reached a level of proficiency had also reached their DEROS date and were rotated. Green troops or ''fucking new guys" with almost no experience in combat were thrown into their places. These FNGs were essentially avoided by the unit, at least until after a few months of experience; "short timers" did not want to get themselves killed by relying on inexperienced replacements. Needless to say, the unit culture or *esprit* was often lost in the lack of communication with the endless leavings and arrivals.

There were other unique aspects of group dynamics in Vietnam. Seasoned troops would stick together, often forming very close small groups for short periods, a normal combat experience noted in previous wars (Grinker and Spiegel, 1945). Some groups formed along racial lines due to lack of unit cohesions within combat outfits. As a seasoned veteran got down to his last two months in Vietnam, he was struck by a strange malady known as the "short timer's syndrome." He would be withdrawn from the field and, if logistically possible, would be settled into a comparatively safe setting for the rest of his tour. His buddies would be left behind in the field without his skills, and he would be left with mixed feelings of joy and guilt. Interestingly, it was rare that a veteran ever wrote to his buddies still in Vietnam once he returned home (Howard, 1976). It has been an even rarer experience for two or more to get together following the war. This is a strong contrast to the endless reunions of World War II veterans. Feelings of guilt about leaving one's buddies to whatever unknown fate in Vietnam apparently proved so strong that many veterans were often too frightened to attempt to find out what happened to those left behind.

Kent State Response, 1970

Another factor unique to the Vietnam War was that the ideological basis for the war was very difficult to grasp. In World War II, the United States was very clearly threatened by a uniformed and easily recognizable foe. In Vietnam, it was quite the opposite. It appeared that the whole country was hostile to American forces. The enemy was rarely uniformed, and American troops were often forced to kill women and children combatants. There were no real lines of demarcation, and just about any area was subject to attack. Most American forces had been trained to fight in conventional warfare, in which other human beings are confronted and a block of land is either acquired or lost in the fray. However, in Vietnam, surprise firing devices such as booby traps accounted for a large number of casualties with the human foe rarely sighted. A block of land might be secured but not held. A unit would pull out to another conflict in the vicinity; and, if it wished to return to the same block of land, it would once again have to fight to take that land. It was an endless war with rarely seen foes and no ground gains, just a constant flow of troops in and out of the country. The only observable outcome was an interminable production of maimed, crippled bodies and countless corpses. Some were so disfigured it was hard to tell if they were Vietnamese or American, but they were all dead. The rage that such conditions generated was widespread among American troops. It manifested itself in violence and mistrust toward the Vietnamese (DeFazio, 1978), toward the authorities, and toward the society that sent these men to Vietnam and then would not support them. Rather than a war with a just ideological basis, Vietnam became a private war of survival for every American individual involved.

What was especially problematic was that this was America's first teenage war (Williams, 1979). The age of the average combatant was close to 20 (Wilson, 1979). According to Wilson (1978), this period for most adolescents involves a psychosocial moratorium (Erikson, 1968), during which the individual takes some time to establish a more stable and enduring personality structure and sense of self. Unfortunately for the adolescents who fought the war, the role of combatant versus survivor, as well as the many ambiguous and conflicting values associated with these roles, led to a clear disruption of this moratorium and to the many subsequent problems that followed for the young veterans.

Many men, who had either used drugs to deal with the overwhelming stresses of combat or developed other behavioral symptoms for similar stress-related etiology, were not recognized as struggling with acute combat reaction or post-traumatic stress disorder, acute subtype. Rather, their immediate behavior had proven to be problematic to the military, and they were offered an immediate resolution in the form of administrative discharges, often with diagnoses of character disorders (Kormos, 1978).

The administrative discharge proved to be another method to temporarily repress any further overt symptoms. It provided yet another means of ending the stress without becoming an actual physical or psychological casualty. It, therefore, served to lower the actual incidence of psychological breakdown, as did the DEROS. Eventually, this widely used practice came to be questioned, and it was recognized that it had been used as a convenient way to eliminate many individuals who had major psychological problems dating from their combat service (Kormos, 1978).

When the veteran finally returned home, his fantasy about his DEROS date was replaced by a rather harsh reality. As previously stated, World War II vets took weeks, sometimes months, to return home with their buddies. Vietnam vets returned home alone. Many made the transition from rice paddy to Southern California in less than 36 hours. The civilian population of the World War II era had been treated to movies about the struggles of readjustment for veterans (i.e., The Man In The Grey Flannel Suit, The Best Years of Our Lives, Pride of the Marines) to prepare them to help the veteran (DeFazio, 1978). The civilian population of the Vietnam era was treated to the horrors of the war on the six o'clock news. They were tired and numb to the whole experience. Some were even fighting mad, and many veterans were witness to this fact. Some World War II veterans came home to victory parades. Vietnam veterans returned in defeat and witnessed antiwar marches and protests. For World War II veterans, resort hotels were taken over and made into redistribution stations to which veterans could bring their wives and devote two weeks to the initial homecoming (Borus, 1973). For Vietnam veterans, there were screaming antiwar crowds and locked military bases where they were processed back into civilian life in two or three days.

Those veterans who were struggling to make it back home finally did. However, they had drastically changed, and their world would never seem the same. Their fantasies were just that: fantasy. What they had experienced in Vietnam and on their return to their homes in the United States would leave an indelible mark that many may never erase.

The Catalysts of Post-Traumatic Stress Disorders for Vietnam Combat Veterans

More than 8.5 million individuals served in the U.S. Armed Forces during the Vietnam era, 1964-1973. Approximately 2.8 million served in Southeast Asia. Of the latter number, almost one million saw active combat or were exposed to hostile, life-threatening situations (President's Commission on Mental Health, 1978). It is this writer's opinion that the vast majority of Vietnam era veterans have had a much more problematic readjustment to civilian life than did their World War II and Korean War counterparts. This was due to the issues already discussed in this chapter, as well as to the state of the economy and the inadequacy of the GI Bill in the early 1970s. In addition, the combat veterans of Vietnam, many of whom immediately tried to become assimilated back into the peacetime culture, discovered that their outlook and feelings about their relationships and future life experiences had changed immensely. According to the fantasy, all was to be well again when they returned from Vietnam. The reality for many was quite different.

Bankruptcy for Breakfast. The newly bankrupt Daniels family—they filed that morning.

A number of studies point out that those veterans subjected to more extensive combat show more problematic symptoms during the period of readjustment (Wilson, 1978; Strayer & Ellenborn, 1975; Kormos, 1978; Shatan, 1978; Figley, 1978). The usual pattern has been that of a combat veteran in Vietnam who held on until his DEROS date. He was largely asymptomatic at the point of his rotation back to the U.S. for the reasons previously discussed; on his return home, the joy of surviving continued to suppress any problematic symptoms. However, after a year or more, the veteran would begin to notice some changes in his outlook (Shatan, 1978). But, because there was a time limit of one year after which the Veterans Administration would not recognize neuropsychiatric problems as service-connected, the veteran was unable to get service-connected disability compensation. Treatment from the VA was very difficult to obtain. The veteran began to feel depressed, mistrustful, cynical and restless. He experienced problems with sleep and with his temper. Strangely, he became somewhat obsessed with his combat experiences in Vietnam. He would also begin to question why he survived when others did not.

For approximately 500,000 veterans (Wilson, 1978) of the combat in Southeast Asia, this problematic outlook has become a chronic lifestyle affecting not only the veterans but countless millions of persons who are in contact with these veterans. The symptoms described below are experienced by all Vietnam combat veterans to varying degrees. However, for some with the most extensive combat histories and other variables which have yet to be enumerated, Vietnam-related problems have persisted in disrupting all areas of life experience. According to Wilson (1978), the number of veterans experiencing these symptoms will climb until 1985, based on his belief of Erickson's psychosocial developmental stages and how far along in these stages most combat veterans will be by 1985. Furthermore, without any intervention, what was once a reaction to a traumatic episode may for many become an almost unchangeable personality characteristic.

The Symptoms of Post-Traumatic Stress Disorder: Chronic and/or Delayed

Depression

The vast majority of the Vietnam combat veterans I have interviewed are depressed. Many have been continually depressed since their experiences in Vietnam. They have the classic symptoms (DSM III, 1980) of sleep disturbance, psychomotor retardation, feelings of worthlessness, difficulty in concentrating, etc. Many of these veterans have weapons in their possession, and they are no strangers to death. In treatment, it is especially important to find out if the veteran keeps a weapon in close proximity, because the possibility of suicide is always present.

When recalling various combat episodes during an interview, the veteran with a post-traumatic stress disorder almost invariably cries. He usually has had one or more episodes in which one of his buddies was killed. When asked how he handled these deaths when in Vietnam, he will often answer, "in the shortest amount of time possible" (Howard, 1976). Due to circumstances of war, extended grieving on the battlefield is very unproductive and could become a liability. Hence, grief was handled as quickly as possible, allowing little or no time for the grieving process. Many men reported feeling numb when this happened. When asked how they are now dealing with the deaths of their buddies in Vietnam, they invariably answer that they are not. They feel depressed; "How can I tell my wife, she'd never understand?" they ask. "How can anyone who hasn't been there understand?" (Howard, 1976).

Accompanying the depression is a very well developed sense of helplessness about one's condition. Vietnam-style combat held no final resolution of conflict for anyone. Regardless of how one might respond, the overall outcome seemed to be just an endless production of casualties with no perceivable goals attained. Regardless of how well one worked, sweated, bled and even died, the outcome was the same. Our GIs gained no ground;

they were constantly rocketed or mortared. They found little support from their "friends and neighbors" back home, the people in whose name so many were drafted into military service. They felt helpless. They returned to the United States, trying to put together some positive resolution of this episode in their lives, but the atmosphere at home was hopeless. They were still helpless. Why even bother anymore?

Many veterans report becoming extremely isolated when they are especially depressed. Substance abuse is often exaggerated during depressive periods. Self medication was an easily learned coping response in Vietnam; alcohol appears to be the drug of choice.

Isolation

Combat veterans have few friends. Many veterans who witnessed traumatic experiences complain of feeling like old men in young men's bodies. They feel isolated and distant from their peers. The veterans feel that most of their non-veteran peers would rather not hear what the combat experience was like; therefore, they feel rejected. Much of what many of these veterans had done during the war would seem like horrible crimes to their civilian peers. But, in the reality faced by Vietnam combatants, such actions were frequently the only means of survival.

Many veterans find it difficult to forget the lack of positive support they received from the American public during the war. This was especially brought home to them on the return from the combat zone to the United States. Many were met by screaming crowds and the media calling them "depraved fiends" and "psychopathic killers" (DeFazio, 1978). Many personally confronted hostility from friends and family, as well as strangers. After their return home, some veterans found that the only defense was to search for a safe place. These veterans found themselves criss-crossing the continent, always searching for that place where they might feel accepted. Many veterans cling to the hope that they can move away from their problems. It is not unusual to interview a veteran who, either alone or with his family, has effectively isolated himself from others by repeatedly moving from one geographical location to another. The stress on his family is immense.

The fantasy of living the life of a hermit plays a central role in many veterans' daydreams. Many admit to extended periods of isolation in the mountains, on the road, or just behind a closed door in the city. Some veterans have actually taken a weapon and attempted to live off the land.

It is not rare to find a combat veteran who has not had a social contact with a woman for years—other than with a prostitute, which is an accepted military procedure in the combat setting. If the veteran does marry, his wife will often complain about the isolation he imposes on the marital situation. The veteran will often stay in the house and avoid any interactions with others. He also resents any interactions that his spouse may initiate. Many times, the wife is the source of financial stability.

Rage

The veterans' rage is frightening to them and to others around them. For no apparent reason, many will strike out at whomever is near. Frequently, this includes their wives and children. Some of these veterans can be quite violent. This behavior generally frightens the veterans, apparently leading many to question their sanity; they are horrified at their behavior. However, regardless of their afterthoughts, the rage reactions occur with frightening frequency.

Often veterans will recount episodes in which they become inebriated and had fantasies that they were surrounded or confronted by enemy Vietnamese. This can prove to be an especially frightening situation when others confront the veteran forcibly. For many combat veterans, it is once again a life-and-death struggle, a fight for survival.

Some veterans have been able to sublimate their rage, breaking inanimate objects or putting fists through walls. Many of them display bruises and cuts on their hands. Often, when these veterans feel the rage emerging, they will immediately leave the scene before somebody or something gets hurt; subsequently, they drive about aimlessly. Quite often, their behavior behind the wheel reflects their mood. A number of veterans have described to me the verbal catharsis they've achieved in explosions of expletives directed at any other drivers who may wrong them.

There are many reasons for the rage. Military training equated rage with masculine identity in the performance of military duty (Eisenhart, 1975). Whether one was in combat or not, the military experience stirred up more resentment and rage than most had ever felt (Egendorf, 1975). Finally, when combat in Vietnam was experienced, the combatants were often left with wild, violent impulses and no one upon whom to level them. The nature of guerrilla warfare—with its use of such tactics as booby trap land mines and surprise ambushes with the enemy's quick retreat—left the combatants feeling like time bombs; the veterans wanted to fight back, but their antagonists had long since disappeared. Often they unleashed their rage at indiscriminate targets for want of more suitable targets (Shatan, 1978).

On return from Vietnam, the rage that had been tapped in combat was displaced against those in authority. It was directed against those the veterans felt were responsible for getting them involved in the war in the first place—and against those who would not support the veterans while they were in Vietnam or when they returned home (Howard, 1976). Fantasies of retaliation against political leaders, the military services, the Veterans Administration and antiwar protesters were present in the minds of many of these Vietnam combat veterans. These fantasies are still alive and generalized to many in the present era.

Along with the rage at authority figures from the Vietnam era, these veterans today often feel a generalized mistrust of anyone in authority and the "system" in the present era. Many combat veterans with stress disorders have a long history of constantly changing their jobs. It is not unusual to interview a veteran who has had 30 to 40 jobs during the past 10 years. One veteran I interviewed had nearly 80 jobs in a 10-year span. The rationale quite often given by the veterans is that they became bored or the work was beneath them. However, after I had made some extended searches into their work background, it became apparent that they felt deep mistrust for their employers and coworkers; they felt used and exploited; at times, such was the case. Many have had some uncomfortable confrontations with their employers and job peers, and many have been fired or have resigned on their own.

Avoidance of Feelings: Alienation

"Silence doesn't work!"

The spouses of many of the veterans I have interviewed complain that the men are cold, uncaring individuals. Indeed, the veterans themselves will recount episodes in which they did not feel anything when they witnessed the death of a buddy in combat or the more recent death of a close family relative. They are often somewhat troubled by these responses to tragedy; but, on the whole, they would rather deal with tragedy in their own detached way. What becomes especially problematic for these veterans, however, is an inability to experience the joys of life. They often described themselves as being emotionally dead (Shatan, 1973).

The evolution of this emotional deadness began for Vietnam veterans when they first entered military boot camp (Shatan, 1973). There they learned that the Vietnamese were not to be labeled as people but as "gooks, dinks, slopes, zipperheads and slants." When the veteran finally arrived in the battle zone, it was much easier to kill a "gook" or "dink" than another human being. This dehumanization gradually generalized to the whole Vietnam experience. The American combatants themselves became "grunts", the Viet-Cong became "Victor Charlie," and both groups were either "KIA" (killed in action) or "WIA" (wounded in action). Often, many "slopes" would get "zapped" (killed) by a "Cobra" (gunship), and the "grunts" would retreat by "Shithook" (evacuation by a Chinook helicopter); the jungle would be sown by "Puff the Magic Dragon" (a C-47 gunship with rapid-firing mini-gatling guns).

The pseudonyms served to blunt the anguish and the horror of the reality of combat (DeFazio, 1978). In conjunction with this almost surreal aspect of the fighting, psychic numbing furthered the coping and survival ability of the combatants by effectively knocking the aspect of feelings out of their cognitive abilities (Lifton, 1976). This defense mechanism of survivors of traumatic experiences dulls an individual's awareness of the death and destruction about him. It is a dynamic survival mechanism, helping one to pass through a period of trauma without becoming caught up in its tendrils. Psychic numbing only becomes nonproductive when the period of trauma is passed, and the individual is still numb to the affect around him.

Many veterans find it extremely uncomfortable to feel love and compassion for others. To do this, they would have to thaw their numb reactions to the death and horror that surrounded them in Vietnam. Some veterans I've interviewed actually believe that if they once again allow themselves to feel, they may never stop crying or may completely lose control of themselves; what they mean by this is unknown to them. Therefore, many of these veterans go through life with an impaired capacity to love and care for others. They have no feeling of direction or purpose in life. They are not sure why they even exist.

Survival Guilt

When others have died and some have not, the survivors often ask, "How is it that I survived when others more worthy than I did not?" (Lifton, 1973). Survival guilt is an especially guilt-invoking symptom. It is not based on anything hypothetical. Rather, it is based on the harshest of realities, the actual death of comrades and the struggle of the survivor to live. Often the survivor has had to compromise himself or the life of someone else in order to live. The guilt that such an act invokes or guilt over simply surviving may eventually end in self-destructive behavior by the survivor.

Many veterans, who have survived when comrades were lost in surpise ambushes, protracted battles of even normal battlefield attrition, exhibit self-destructive behavior. It is common for them to recount the combat death of someone they held in esteem; and, invariably, the question comes up, "Why wasn't it me?" It is not unusual for these men to set themselves up for hopeless physical fights with insurmountable odds. "I don't know why, but I always pick the biggest guy," said the veteran in the transcript at the beginning of this chapter. Shatan (1973) notes that some of these men become involved in repeated single-car auto accidents. This writer interviewed one surviving veteran, whose company suffered over 80% casualties in one ambush. The veteran had had three single-car accidents during the previous week, two the day before he came in for the interview. He was wondering if he were trying to kill himself.

I have also found that those veterans who suffer the most painful survival guilt are primarily those who served as corpsmen or medics. These unfortunate veterans were trained for a few months to render first aid on the actual field of battle. The services they individually performed were heroic. With a bare amount of medical knowledge and large amounts of courage and determination, they saved countless lives. However, many of the men they tried to save died. Many of these casualties were beyond all medical help, yet many corpsmen and medics suffer extremely painful memories to this day, blaming their "incompetence" for these deaths. Listening to these veterans describe their anguish and torment...seeing the

Missing Vet Series. Keeping a phone-side vigil, Marilyn awaits word of her suicide threatening husband.

heroin tracks up and down their arms or the bones that have been broken in numerous barroom fights...is, in itself, a very painful experience.

Another less destructive trend that I have noticed exists among a small number of Vietnam combat veterans who have become compulsive blood donors. One very isolated and alienated individual I interviewed actually drives some 80 miles round-trip once every other month to make his donation. His military history reveals that he was one of 13 men out of a 60-man platoon who survived the battle of Hue. He was the only survivor who was not wounded. This veteran and similar vets talk openly about their guilt, and they find some relief today in giving their blood that others may live.

Anxiety Reactions

Many Vietnam veterans describe themselves as very vigilant human beings; their autonomic senses are tuned to anything out of the ordinary. A loud discharge will cause many of them to start. A few will actually take such evasive action as falling to their knees or to the ground. Many veterans become very uncomfortable when people walk closely behind them. One veteran described his discomfort when people drive directly behind him. He would pull off the road, letting others pass, when they got within a few car lengths of him.

Some veterans are uncomfortable when standing out in the open. Many are uneasy when sitting with others behind them, often opting to sit up against something solid, such as a wall. The bigger the object is, the better. Many combat veterans are most comfortable when sitting in the corner in a room, where they can see everyone about them. Needless to say, all of these behaviors are learned survival techniques. If a veteran feels continuously threatened, it is difficult for him to give such behavior up.

A large number of veterans possess weapons. This also is a learned survival technique. Many still sleep with weapons in easy reach. The uneasy feeling of being caught asleep is apparently very difficult to master once having left the combat zone.

Sleep Disturbance and Nightmares

Few veterans struggling with post-traumatic stress disorders find the hours immediately before sleep very comfortable. In fact, many will stay awake as long as possible. They will often have a drink or smoke some cannabis to dull any uncomfortable cognition that may enter during this vulnerable time period. Many report that they have nothing to occupy their minds at the end of the day's activities, and their thoughts wander. For many of them, it is a trip back to the battle zone. Very often they will watch TV late into the mornings.

Missing Vet Series. Searching for her husband is taking its toll on Marilyn Watson.

Finally, with sleep, many veterans report having dreams about being shot at or being pursued and left with an empty weapon, unable to run anymore. Recurrent dreams of specific traumatic episodes are frequently reported, it is not unusual for a veteran to reexperience, night after night, the death of a close friend or a death that he caused as a combatant. Dreams of everyday, common experiences in Vietnam are also frequently reported. For many, just the fear that they might actually be back in Vietnam is very disquieting.

Some veterans report being unable to remember their specific dreams, yet they feel dread about them. Wives and partners report that the men sleep fitfully, and some call out in agitation. A very few actually grab their partners and attempt to do them harm before they have fully awakened. Finally, maintaining sleep has proven to be a problem for many of these veterans. They report waking up often during the night for no apparent reason. Many rise quite early in the morning, still feeling very tired.

Intrusive Thoughts

Traumatic memories of the battlefield and other less affect-laden combat experiences often play a role in the daytime cognitions of combat veterans. Frequently, these veterans report replaying especially problematic combat experiences over and over again. Many search for possible alternative outcomes to what actually happened in Vietnam. Many castigate themselves for what they might have done to change the situation, suffering subsequent guilt feelings today because they were unable to do so in combat. The vast majority report that these thoughts are very uncomfortable, yet they are unable to put them to rest.

Many of the obsessive episodes are triggered by common, everyday experiences that remind the veteran of the war zone: helicopters flying overhead, the smell of urine (corpses have no muscle tone, and the bladder evacuates at the moment of death), the smell of diesel fuel (the commodes and latrines contained diesel fuel and were burned when filled with human excrement), green tree lines (these were searched for any irregularity which often meant the presence of enemy movement), the sound of popcorn popping (the sound is very close to that of small arms gunfire in the distance), any loud discharge, a rainy day (it rains for months during the monsoons in Vietnam) and finally the sight of Vietnamese refugees.

A few combat veterans find the memories invoked by some of these and other stimuli so uncomfortable that they will actually go out of their way to avoid them. When exposed to one of the above or similar stimuli, a very small number of combat veterans undergo a short period of time in a dissociative-like state in which they actually reexperience past events in Vietnam. These flashbacks can last anywhere from a few seconds to a few hours. One veteran described an episode to me in which he had seen some armed men and felt he was back in Vietnam. The armed men were police officers. Not having a weapon to protect himself and others, he grabbed a passerby and forcefully sheltered this person in his home to protect him from what he felt were the "gooks." Needless to say, the passerby screamed, and the police stormed the house. The veteran was incoherent when they finally reached him, yelling about "the damn gooks." He was medicated and hospitalized for a week.

Such experiences among Vietnam veterans are rare, but not as uncommon as many may believe. Many veterans report flashback episodes that last only a few seconds. For many, the sound of a helicopter flying overhead is a cue to forget reality for a few seconds and remember Vietnam reexperiencing feelings they had there. It is especially troublesome for those veterans who are still "numb" and specifically attempting to avoid these feelings. For others, it is just a constant reminder of their time in Vietnam, something they will never forget.

Reprinted from *Post-Traumatic Stress Disorders of the Vietnam Veteran*, edited by Tom Williams, DAV, 1980©. Permission for reprint: Disabled American Veterans.

Jim Goodwin, Psy.D. is a Marine combat veteran of the Vietnam War. In a single year, Goodwin conducted more than 300 intakes for the DAV's outreach program in Denver, where he served as a group co-leader in the project for more than a year. Goodwin was responsible for writing Chapter I of the book *Post-Traumatic Stress Disorders of the Vietnam Veteran*, published by the Disabled American Veterans and distributed free (approximately 50,000 copies) to mental health and other counseling professionals. Goodwin has re-entered the Armed Forces, where he continues his work with veterans.

Fountain's Fear. Downcast eyes in overcast times. A Cincinnati fountain is adorned with the black armband of Moratorium Day, 1969.

Reaching out to Troubled Vietnam Vets: The Dav's Role
Tom Keller and Jerry Atchison

In the mid-'70s, statistics began describing what the veteran could not. Suddenly it was apparent to almost everyone in the land that, as a group, Vietnam veterans were experiencing some real problems.

At about this same time, John P. Wilson, PhD., a psychologist from Cleveland (Ohio) State University, was tramping from one government agency to another, looking for funding of research to get at the root of the veterans' problems.

Previously, small-scale studies had hinted at the nature of the readjustment problems the veterans were experiencing. Dr. Wilson now proposed a larger, comprehensive study of the problem. He planned a study that, finally, would begin answering some of the perplexing questions facing the Vietnam veteran.

In short order, the non-profit Disabled American Veterans (DAV) funded Dr. Wilson's study and launched his research efforts. The results of that study, dubbed The Forgotten Warrior Project, contained revelations that shocked even health care professionals.

The research demonstrated that combat-related flash-backs and nightmares were far more common than anyone could have imagined. Self-destructive behavior was indeed a problem for veterans who felt unjustified but persistent guilt. Withdrawal from family, friends and life in general was showing up with appalling frequency, as were isolation, alienation, loneliness, depression, rage, anxiety neuroses and an inability to cope with a wide variety of life situations.

Dr. Wilson's study also found that the symptoms varied greatly in number and intensity from one veteran to the next, but the common thread was participation in guerrilla combat in Vietnam. Further, the more extensive the combat exposure, the more severe the symptoms.

The curious malady afflicting Vietnam veterans began to take form through Dr. Wilson's research. Other studies in related research fields combined with the Forgotten Warrior Project began adding up: there were several problems here, problems that were definable and that were widespread and life-threatening. But—importantly—they were problems that were treatable and curable.

Despite this information, neither Congress nor the Veterans Administration (VA) would address these problems. Legislation had been introduced in Congress to establish a network of outreach offices that would use group therapy techniques. These techniques had demonstrated levels of success with post-traumatic stress in the few, local, self-help projects that existed at the time for Vietnam veterans.

Congress refused to act because they demanded proof that serious readjustment problems existed and that they could be cured. Yet when the DAV provided that proof in the form of Dr. Wilson's Forgotten Warrior Project and other research efforts, Congress turned a deaf ear to the cure. And if Congressional ears go deaf, it can reasonably be expected that the same will happen within the VA.

It was then that the DAV set out to professionally staff a nationwide network of store front centers to aid the Vietnam veteran suffering from post-traumatic stress.

It became an immense task that required one-fourth of the DAV's national service officers (NSOs) to be taken out of their offices to staff storefront offices in 68 cities and several satellite locations. These NSOs would also have to quickly transform themselves into something akin to psychological social workers, a role only vaguely familiar to most of them.

Huge amounts of money were required to pay the salaries and benefits of the 70 NSOs and the clerical support they required. An additional $1 million was raised to make the outreach concept work.

A whole new nationwide relationship between DAV NSOs and mental health professionals was needed in order to secure the volunteer psychiatrists and psychologists the DAV needed to run the group therapy sessions, which came to be known as "rap groups."

Developing the required network of outreach offices turned the DAV inside-out, shaking the organization to its very roots and raising serious doubts among its members as to whether it could succeed.

But, within six months, pilot programs in six cities were up and running. And within a year, DAV Vietnam Veterans Outreach Program offices were open in the remaining 62 cities.

And Vietnam veterans—troubled that their lives had gone seriously awry—began flocking to the outreach centers across the nation. Vietnam veterans, as a group, began throwing off the yokes of guilt that had burdened their progress for years. They were openly discussing their feelings about the war, feelings many had never discussed with anyone before.

The program was proving therapeutic for the people of the United States too. The publicity generated by the DAV Vietnam Veterans Outreach Program forced the United States public to take a new look at the war...to deal with their own long-repressed feelings about it. And the program finally proved to Congress and the White House that the outreach concept worked.

A year after the DAV initiated its program, Congress passed legislation authorizing the VA's "Operation Outreach," which was modeled after the DAV's program.

But the DAV's job did not end when the federal government program began. As pioneers in the identification and treatment of post-traumatic stress in Vietnam veterans, DAV experts were called upon to teach their skills to others in the mental health care fields. These experts conducted more than 100 formal seminars for mental health and other counseling professionals, helping them learn the subtle skills that permit one to trace the stress disorders to their combat roots and begin the healing process.

Tom Keller and Jerry Atchison both served as military journalists during the Vietnam War. Keller met and worked with photographer Gordon Baer in the Republic of Korea, where they had been sent as part of the U.S. Air Force troop build-up following the North Korean capture of the *U.S.S. Pueblo*. Atchison, a U.S. Navy veteran, served in Vietnam in 1972. Keller is Assistant National Director of Communication at the National Headquarters of the Disabled American Veterans, where Atchison serves as Associate National Director of Communications.

Operation Outreach for Vietnam Veterans
Arthur S. Blank, Jr., M.D.

On June 13, 1979, President Carter signed Public Law 96-22 authorizing the Veterans Administration to form a new system to provide readjustment counseling for Vietnam veterans with psychological problems derived from duty in the war. The result is a nationwide network of Vietnam vet centers—collectively termed Operation Outreach—in all 50 states, Puerto Rico, and the Virgin Islands. These centers have been set up outside existing VA medical facilities (although they receive administrative support from them) and treat veterans with a broad range of individual and group counseling (rap groups) and family counseling, and offer assistance with problems in employment, education, and VA benefits.

As of August 1982, the centers had seen well over 125,000 Vietnam-era veterans and tens of thousands of family members. By October 1983, the centers have treated approximately 200,000 veterans and made 170,000 visits with family members. These figures may be just the beginning. It recently was discovered that up to 4 million Americans, not 3 million or less as had been believed, may have served in Indochina between 1964 and 1975. Most research indicates that at least 20 percent of Vietnam veterans have substantial war-related psychological difficulties that are impairing their lives. Thus the program has a potential clientele of some 700,000 to 800,000 veterans plus family members. In 1981, legislation continuing the programs was passed unanimously by both houses of Congress and signed by President Reagan. The most recent legislation passed by both houses of Congress and signed by the President in 1983 extends this program until 1988. This new legislation also includes lifetime eligibility for re-adjustment counseling from the VA for Vietnam-era veterans.

Today there are 136 vet centers operating nationwide, an increase of 45 since the program began in 1979. In fiscal 1982, its budget was increased by some $9 million in a time when many federal budgets were being cut drastically. However, the program still has a staff of only about 560 to serve a population of more than 800,000.

Reprinted from "Apocalypse Terminable and Interminable: Operation Outreach for Vietnam Veterans," *Hospital and Community Psychiatry*, 33, November 1982©. Permission to reprint: *Hospital and Community Psychiatry.*

Arthur S. Blank, Jr., M.D. is the Director of Readjustment Counseling Service, Veterans Administration, Washington, D.C. and a recognized authority on the diagnosis and treatment of post-traumatic stress disorders. Dr. Blank served as a psychiatric medical officer in Vietnam. Prior to his present post in Washington, he was a member of the psychiatric staff at the New Haven VA Medical Center.

The Postwar Healing of Vietnam Veterans: Psychological Implications of Recent Research
Arthur Egendorf, Ph.D.

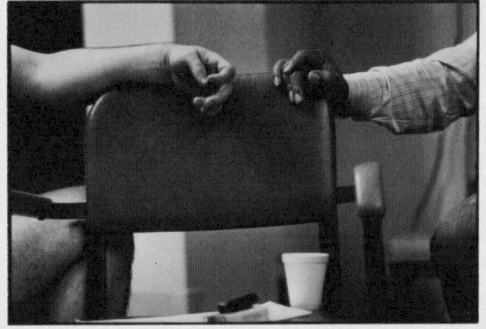

Brothers in outreach.

The growing body of research on Vietnam veterans provides an alternative to long-standing stereotypes. Prejudiced views include the media image of veterans as "drug-crazed baby killers" as well as the more subtly denigrating notions that dismiss all veteran problems as artifacts of prewar disposition (the "bad apple" theory), or that lump all veterans together as objects of sympathy, pitiable victims of an immoral war. A more accurate portrait, and one that serves postwar healing, would emphasize the following four correctives.

First, it is time to lay to rest the question of whether the aftermath of the Vietnam war differed from the aftermath of other wars. It is both the same and different. In all wars people are killed, maimed, and traumatized. All wars bring about deep social and historical ruptures that intrude on individual lives in ways that cannot be ignored by those affected or by others who want to understand them. A historically relevant analysis would also examine the unique aspects of the Vietnam War and how those aspects influence recovery among veterans.

For example, many observers have said that long-term prospects for recovery and healing among Vietnam veterans have been hampered by the enduring controversies surrounding the war, and because it ended in an American defeat. Just as crucial, if less seldom noted, are recent and momentous global developments. The moon landings, high-speed computers, and satellite technology have made into a commonplace notion the ancient dream of a world that communicates as a unified human family. At the same time, armed conflict in the nuclear era raises the specter of human self-extinction. Veterans, like everybody who has been buffeted by historic upheaval, live with "the world too much with us." The difficult task of reconciling the incomparable promise and the unprecedented threat of our era complicates the healing process for veterans, who tend to be more personally caught up in the historic issues of their time than the average person their age.

The second corrective is to cease oversimplifying public and professional portrayals of the veteran experience. We need, instead, to recognize the wide variation among Vietnam veterans. Even the "stress response" is not one response to the war, but a range of responses, the quality of which varies not only with prewar experiences, with socioeconomic, ethnic, and racial background, and with the nature of duty and involvement in Vietnam but also with a host of experience and structural aspects of veterans' postwar lives. Whatever is said about veterans, and particularly whatever therapeutic interventions are undertaken, should take into account this range of responses.

As a third corrective, mental health professionals should heed the evidence about psychopathology. A definable symptom cluster can be linked, statistically, with war experiences, and this condition calls for more treatment and studies of the efficacy of such treatment. It is important to emphasize, however, that diagnosable conditions occur only among a minority of veterans. The relative ease of identifying this minority should not obscure the far more pervasive problem: the subclinical malaise that afflicts more than two million men, a virtual majority of those who served.

More recognition should be given to this majority of veterans who are not suffering from a clear disorder but who could benefit greatly from some form of intervention. At their most optimistic, designers of the new VA outreach program hope to reach 75,000 veterans per year. Clearly, the postwar malaise is too widespread and too diffuse to be addressed solely through existing programs. Resources other than those that are part of the official mental health system may need to be tapped. I have met scores of veterans who have increased their inner strength by studying meditative disciplines, and through taking courses to enhance "human potential." For some, the self-discipline cultivated in martial arts training has been useful. I have found one educational innovation, the *est* training, to be unusually well suited in content and tone for helping former soldiers to meet more fully the challenges of civilian life.

As a fourth and final corrective, much more thought and attention should be given to the possibilities for further healing. This is the most far-reaching recommendation and warrants more extensive comment than the others.

Healing Work with Veterans

Professional discussions and reports in popular media have rarely noted the striking therapeutic changes already exhibited by the increasing minority of veterans who are not merely adjusting but thriving. This minority includes prominent veteran advocates. The phenomenon has been captured in the title *Strong at the Broken Places* (Cleland, 1980), a book written by Max Cleland, Vietnam veteran, triple amputee, and recent administrator of veterans affairs for the VA.

The possibilities for further healing will become more apparent only as the discussion of postwar stress takes on more subtlety and rigor. Rather than conceiving of postwar stress as an accretion of "past stressors" on passive objects, clinical experience suggests that we take account of the "reflexive" nature of human experience. Within this perspective, the significance of the past is linked to the way people currently engage or fail to engage it. Thus war experiences need not have a fixed effect on veterans' lives. Even the incidents we properly designate as traumatic need not remain permanently devastating; veterans always have the option of working through their conflicts, by way of therapy or developmental changes that take place outside the clinic.

Change of this sort is, of course, always embedded in a social context. For Vietnam veterans in general, the data show that those who have gone furthest in working through their personal legacy of the war seem not only to have reflected on their war experience but have talked considerably about it with others who support their explorations. Most often their confidante has been a lover or wife with whom they have established a fulfilling, intimate relationship. The limited progress of other veterans may reveal as much about the tendency among their family and friends toward avoidance, blame, and resignation to guilt and trauma as it does about the veterans themselves.

It is therefore important to supplement and provide alternatives to exclusively individual treatment, by including partners, families, and support groups of other veterans as well as courses in life enhancement and development of human potential as part of on-going programs.

It is just as crucial to see that the proper context in which to address postwar healing extends beyond a focus on veterans and their families. In summarizing the results of the *Legacies of Vietnam* study, two of my colleagues and I wrote that the Vietnam War is unfinished business for the entire generation that came of age during that time. Most Americans still find it difficult to talk openly with each other about the events of the war years. Many men who served in the military think that others neither know nor want to understand what the war was actually like. Nonveterans are often constrained by a mixture of sympathy and envy for exsoldiers, along with a sense of relief tinged with guilt that they themselves were spared. To address the need for healing in this broader social context, mental health professionals and spiritual and political leaders should promote reconciliation throughout the community by using the popular media and other public education channels.

The Wider Healing

Two facets of this wider healing are worth noting here. First, we need to develop a new public attitude; people should be encouraged to feel, reflect on, and speak about unresolved experiences of the war and to be responsive to others' attempts to do the same. Vast stores of bitterness, pain, and fierce resentment may need to be voiced and heard without rancor, so that people are less bound inwardly by emotions and memories they previously felt were inexpressible. As part of this new attitude, former combatants and all the rest of us have to forgive ourselves for Vietnam—for the massive suffering and loss, for the wrongs to each other, and for the colossal blow to our national pride—before we can hope to speak and listen clearly to each other as we discuss the honest differences that will always be with us.

Much the way "individual growth" and "human potential" became widely celebrated notions during an earlier decade, "community healing" should now come into vogue. Rather than being used to gloss over our difficulties, community healing should generate possibilities for more satisfactory ways of living together. Only by beginning what appears to be a widely impossible task will we ever resolve the unfinished business of the war.

The second, equally crucial aspect of healing is the need for people to re-engage themselves responsibly with aspects of collective life that many have shunned in recent years. Along with the dead and the wounded, our sense of national purpose became a major casualty of the war. The problem takes such varied forms as suspiciousness of leaders, decreasing trust in public institutions, dwindling voter participation and economic productivity, and a diminished willingness to pull together toward common goals. This generational malaise will be surmounted only through efforts that bring people together from different sides of the rifts associated with the war—old and young, veterans and nonveterans, hawks and doves—in activities that enhance a sense of community and shared purpose.

Among veterans such increased engagement has already begun to happen. Observers of the early veterans' rap groups often commented that the opportunity to "do something useful" was as vital to participants as the social and psychological functions of the group process itself. Informally I have noted an increasing tendency for ex-soldiers to "get involved," whether through joining one of the new veterans' organizations such as Vietnam Veterans of America or volunteering as helpers in VA hospitals or other community programs. The new Vietnam Veteran Leadership Program, run by ACTION, the agency that directs the Peace Corps and VISTA, has also officially recognized the importance of advancing ways for veterans to contribute to each other and to their communities. As a consultant to various programs, I have encouraged veterans to involved themselves in settings that provide them with services. In hospitals such a contribution might be as simple as forming committees to help with routine tasks on their own or neighboring wards.

Constructive action to further communal objectives was once called service, before the majority of the Vietnam generation felt vindicated for having avoided or said "no" to service, and before many individuals who risked their lives became embittered for having voiced a willing or grudging "yes." But the desire to contribute to society and promote the general welfare still exists among the generation that fought in and against the war. This desire needs to be recognized and fostered among veterans and nonveterans alike so that a healthy pride in citizenship, a *sine qua non* of vital communities, can reawaken.

Reprinted from "The Postwar Healing of Vietnam Veterans: Recent Research," *Hospital and Community Psychiatry*, 33, November 1982©. Permission for reprint: *Hospital and Community Psychiatry*.

Arthur Egendorf received a B.A. in economics from Harvard College and studied at L'Institut d'Etudes Politiques in Paris before serving with U.S. Army Intelligence in Vietnam and Washington, D.C. After the war he received a Ph.D. in clinical psychology from Yeshiva University. From 1970 to 1974 he coordinated the Vietnam veteran rap groups in New York City and then initiated the Vietnam Era Research Project, which was selected in 1978 to fulfill a Congressional mandate for a nationwide study of the war's impact on the men of the Vietnam generation. He is completing a book on healing work with ex-soldiers, to be published in 1985. He practices psychotherapy and lives in New York City, with Sondra, his wife, and Sara, his daughter.

What the Vietnam Vets can Teach us
Peter Marin

The dedication of the Vietnam veterans' memorial on the Washington Mall two weeks ago aroused the familiar controversies about its design and its cultural and political functions, echoing many of the points of view about the war that remain among us. There is very little one can say about the monument itself. Its clean lines demand contemplation rather than patriotism or veneration, and perhaps no one can argue with that; but they do very little to remind Americans about the actual nature of the Vietnam War—the horrors and corruption, the moral culpability and negligence, the excesses—or about their own country.

One cannot be surprised by that, of course. Roland Barthes pointed out long ago that a culture's myths serve two functions at once: they commemorate the past but also disguise it, they make it both more and less than it was, they erode history and with it the palpable truths of specific human action and its consequences. It is much the same with monuments or memorials. These are the material ways societies mythologize the past, making it a part of memory rather than thought, an object of sentiment rather than sentience. The Vietnam memorial is no exception, and the fact that we do the same thing in America makes us no worse than anyone else; one can hardly expect images of napalmed children and weeping parents to remind us of what the war was really like. And it is true, too, that there are so many veterans currently in one sort of distress or another that one ought not to be overly scrupulous about anything that may, like the memorial, alleviate it.

And yet, having said that, one must say something more. It would be unfortunate for us all, including the veterans, if the memorial had the effect of closing the door on the past or trying to heal the wounds left behind—as if, in the words of a veteran I met recently, "everything was all right now, all hunky-dory, we're all friends again and all that shit, and the war itself

Vietnam pervades a family's 4th of July celebration, 1967.

Weapons for Peace, 1969.

will be forgotten." For we have not, as a people, really come to terms with the moral questions raised by the war or understood the lessons it ought to have taught us. And we have not begun to come to terms with what the vets are only now, as the war gradually recedes into the past, beginning to learn about themselves and can perhaps teach the rest of us.

That is why it seems to me important not to worry too much about the memorial's design, nor even to concentrate on the horrors of war and the plight of the vets, but rather to reflect upon the knowledge and wisdom that at least a few men have begun in private to mine from the war. I cannot speak here about all vets, or even most of them, so I will concentrate on the men I met this September in Rochester at the first New York State convention of the Vietnam Veterans of America, which I was invited to attend because of what I had previously written about veterans. Technically, what I have to say applies only to the 300 or so vets at the convention, and obviously it is not true of all vets. The V.V.A. as an organization is rather radical, or at least its leaders and several of its chapters are, but even among its members there are many different attitudes toward the past; many of the men are antiwar and antigovernment, but many others believe (or try to believe) that the war was necessary and just and their own roles justifiable. Yet whatever their differences, they have certain characteristics in common; and I have met enough other vets to know that there must be countless others like them scattered across the country, and that what I saw in Rochester must be going on elsewhere.

What impresses me most about the vets I know is the sensibility that has emerged among them in recent years; a particular kind of moral seriousness which is unusual in America, one which is deepened and defined by the fact that it has emerged from a direct confrontation not only with the capacity of others for violence and brutality but also with their own culpability, their sense of their own capacity for error and excess. Precisely the same kinds of experiences that have produced in some vets the complex constellations of panic from which they seem unable to recover have engendered in others an awareness of moral complexity and human tragedy unlike anything one is likely to find elsewhere in America today.

It is this underlying seriousness, I think, that accounts among other effects, for the ways these veterans treat one another. Whatever their behavior—and it is often skeptical, joking, an affectionate roughhousing—there remains an undercurrent of easygoing and generous concern, or care, or what one might even call (how one hesitates to use the word) love.

I remember two instances of it in particular. The first was a talk given by Gary Beikirch, a Medal of Honor winner who is now president of the Genesee Valley V.V.A. chapter. He described his sense of isolation and humiliation in the years after the war, somehow intensified by the medal he had gotten (so much for the dream that "appreciation" will make the vets feel better). And then he talked about what it had been like to make tentative contact with the vets in the Rochester group and to discover among them the camaraderie he needed. What he described was a kind of healing similar to that which some vets in outreach programs and "rap" groups have provided for one another.

The second occasion was the appearance, at the start of the final night's dinner, of a black vet who had apparently walked in off the street uninvited with his wife and child in tow. He made his way to the microphone and, while brandishing a baseball bat, began to speak: "I ain't here to make trouble, I don't wanna have any trouble, but I gotta tell you, I need help. I got a wife, a kid, I got no job, I don't belong anywhere, there's no one will give me any help..." The vets to a man had been tensed for trouble, but now, suddenly, two or three came up to him and led him to a table and invited his wife and child to join them, and he became part of their group. And at the microphone Bobby Muller, the national V.V.A. head, whose turn it was to speak, smiled and said from his wheelchair, "Listen, bro, you're gonna come to our big convention next year in Washington, you hear me? But that's a big one, so bring more than a baseball bat. You'll need your heavy artillery."

These are vets who have, quite literally, brought one another back from the dead, often saved one another from suicide. Their relationships are full of a tenderness and generosity that is rare among American men—at least in public. (Sometimes they themselves are blissfully unaware of it; at others, when they notice it, they seem astonished.) I cannot remember seeing anything like it save among black college students in the late 1960s or among civil rights workers and elderly blacks in the South or—oddly enough—among the members of a fraternity to which I belonged in the 1950s, who seemed, beyond all rhetoric, to be genuinely brotherly toward one another.

It is this capacity for generosity, this kind of learned concern, which colors their moral sensibility, as if there were still at work in them a moral yearning or innocence that had somehow been deepened, rather than destroyed, by the war. A few days after I came home from my stay with the vets, a friend asked me: "Well, what is it they really want?" And I said, without thinking, "Justice." That is what they want, but it is not justice for themselves—though they would like that too. They simply want justice to exist, for there to be justice in the world: some moral order, a moral order maintained by other man and women one can trust. Their yearning is made all the more poignant by the fact that they still do not understand that if justice is to exist, they will have to be the ones who *create* rather than receive it. They do not yet—not *yet*—see it as their own work, not because they are lazy, but simply because it is not a role they associate with themselves. Like most Americans, they do not have a sense of themselves as makers and sustainers of moral values, even though, without knowing it, that is what many of them have become.

I remember how, at the closing banquet, the vets rose and applauded each speaker, moved by the sentiments they heard. There came a moment

Nothing left untouched.

when a former South Vietnamese major, attending the convention uninvited, came up to the dais to offer a plaque to Gary Beikirch. He said that someday the vets would have to return to Vietnam to finish the job they had started but had been forced to stop. Without thinking, on cue, the whole room stood and applauded, the vets and their wives and friends and guests. Yet is was obviously not a sentiment most of them really shared, and later they laughed sheepishly about their enthusiasm. What is revealed was how susceptible the vets are—as, in a sense we all are—to rhetoric and ritual and what the moment seems to demand. It is, paradoxically, the vets' yearning for goodness, for something to believe, which fuels their desire for justice but also makes them vulnerable to rhetoric and ritual, just as it did long ago when they went off to war.

One must remember: these were the good children. Several of them had fathers who served in World War II and passed on to them a sense of obligation and a belief in glory of war. Many others—a surprising number, in fact, were Catholics who were inspired at an early age by John Kennedy's call to "ask what you can do for your country" in fighting Communism (one must not forget how rigorously at the time American Catholicism was intent on confronting Communism everywhere), they would satisfy not only their parents, teachers, and priests but also God and the Pope and the President—all at once. They were, in short, those whose faith in their elders, and in American myth and the American order of things, was so strong, so innocent, that war seemed beyond all doubt a good thing, a form of virtue.

And largely because their belief was so strong at the start—not only in the war but in all authority—their disillusionment and subsequent sense of loss were much stronger. One is tempted to call this an "orphan effect." They were cut off from any sustaining world. Church, state, parents, politicians, Army officers—all the hierarchical sources of moral truth and authority dissolved around them during the war, leaving them exposed without consolation to the stark facts of human culpability and brutality. I remember a remark I heard a vet make a year or two ago. He had said that he wondered if the Vietnamese people would ever forgive him for what he did. When someone asked whether he worried about God forgiving him, he answered, "My problem is that I haven't yet learned how to forgive God."

When I am asked, as I often am, why the Vietnam War so much affected—and so adversely affected—these young men, I am always surprised by the question, because the answers seem to be so obvious.

In the first place, it is probable that all wars have devastating effects upon the men they use—and these were not men when they fought but adolescents, averaging just about 19 years of age. It is hard to believe that something similar to what the soldiers in Vietnam felt was not felt by the men involved in the pointless horrors of trench warfare in World War I; and I cannot help thinking about what one vet told me in Rochester about his father and World War II:

"He never talked much about it except for the usual glorious things, about service to the country and becoming a man. But every year, on New Year's Day, he would lock himself into his den and get dead drunk. He never explained why he did it, but I think now he was remembering the war and mourning. Once, just once, after I got back from Nam, he asked me what it was like, and then he began talking about his war and what he had seen and how it had felt, the killing and the death, and he didn't really feel very much different about it than I did about Nam. It was simply that he had kept it to himself."

For another thing, although what happened to many men in Vietnam did happen to other men in other wars, the cumulative psychological effects were much greater. War, to be sure, is hell, but the effects of this one were compounded by its specific characteristics, as witnessed by the fact that a higher percentage of veterans emerged from this war with psychological disturbances than, as far as we know, from any previous war. (Without question, the rate of suicide and attempted suicide is higher among Vietnam vets than among those of other wars.) Moreover, the attention paid to the damages wrought upon the veterans by this war has been much greater than in the past.

There are other elements that make the Vietnam War different from and even worse than other wars. Even now most Americans do not realize the extent to which it was marked by arbitrary killing and the murder of civilians—out of either official policy or the casual, recreational or simply half-mad behavior of individual men apparently subject to neither internal nor external constraint. It was a war in which innocents became fair game and in which our soldiers—who went to war convinced they were saviors and guardians of freedom—found themselves perceived by the civilian population as intruders, conquerers and even murderers. Their military leaders at several levels of command proved to be venal, dishonest or stupid, and everywhere around them flourished forms of American corruption and vice—black-marketeering, profiteering, thievery—which most of them had never seen close up before. It was a bad war fought for all the wrong reasons and in all the wrong ways, and one could hardly avoid seeing that after being in it for a short while. All of the death, and all of the risk, and even all of the camaraderie and bravery that mark the lives of soldiers anywhere, even those engaged in wrong causes—all of that was rendered meaningless and unnecessary because the war itself was so obviously a bad one.

And there is, finally, one other reason for the Vietnam vets' special pain: we have, as a people, and largely without knowing it, shifted our attitudes toward war, outgrowing the ease with which we may once have accepted violence. Cultures do grow up; just as certain moral attitudes can atrophy, others can develop. Many Americans are no longer able to accept without question or horror the nature of war, indeed, it may well be that in future wars (save for the most obviously self-defensive) many combatants will feel, afterward, what the vets now feel about Vietnam. In short, the vets may be experienced, as their *individual* pain, the half conscious tensions and confusions that Americans, as a society, now bring to violence and war.

Therefore, more than veterans of any other wars past what these men have been forced to confront is *their own capacity for error*; they understand that whatever they experienced—the horror, the terror—has its roots and complements in their own weaknesses and mistakes. For them all conversation about human error or evil is a conversation about themselves; they are pushed past smug ideology and the condemnation of others to an examination of the world that is an examination of self. They know there is no easy relation between one's self-image and the consequences of one's actions. They know too that whatever truths one holds at any given moment will turn out to be if not mistaken then at least incomplete, and that often one's opponents or antagonists will turn out to have been more right than one thought and probably as serious in intention as oneself. Because they cannot easily divide the world into two camps, and because they cannot easily claim virtue while ascribing evil to others, they inhabit a moral realm more complex than the one in which most others live. They know that a moral life means an acknowledgment of guilt as well as a claim to virtue, and they have learned—oh, hardest lesson of all—to judge their own actions in terms of their irrevocable consequences to others.

This sense of moral complexity seems to me to put to shame much of the rhetoric and ethical carelessness that marks America's political life. On both the left and the right, there is a puritanical zealousness attached to almost every position, a moral provincialism in the midst of which people become magically assured of their own virtue and their opponents' culpability and knavery, no matter what the issue or how complicated the questions involved. It hardly matters whether one is speaking to a conservative who favors abortion or a liberal who opposes it, to a proponent of nuclear energy or someone against it. People seem to believe beyond all question that they speak somehow for God and Truth, and that anyone who holds a different view is not only wrong but also less humane, less human, allied with the Devil. Moral hysteria and smugness triumph on every side; Jane Fonda's liberal heroines in film after film are as hollowly virtuous, as unmitigatedly pure, as John Wayne's heroes ever were. The complexities and ironies of truth and half-truth and the ambiguities of moral experience are crushed under the weight of assurance and attitudinizing. One has the feeling that the Jacobins reign supreme and that one's own side, in power, would be no more humane or generous than the side to which it is opposed.

Not so with the vets—that is what I love about them.

But this moral depth, this seriousness, may well go to waste—that is what is most poignant about it. The vets for the most part remain so isolated, so locked into their own pain, that there are few avenues for what is within them to make its way into the larger world, or be sustained and refined by the larger world. If someone somewhere would take the trouble

The Silent War Rages On.

to draw forth from the veterans what it is they feel, think and know, or to convince them to speak, all of us would be better off.

It is probably true, as Karl Jaspers pointed out almost four decades ago in talking to the German people about guilt, that people can look closely at their own moral guilt only when others around them are willing to consider their lives in the same way. This is precisely what the vets have been denied, and therefore their seriousness—which ought to afford them entrance into the larger world, connecting them to all those others who have thought about and suffered similar things—does not. They cannot locate men or women willing to take them as seriously as they take the questions that plague them.

That is what seems so wasteful, and there is something almost unforgiveable about it. I have seen similar kinds of waste over and over in America during the past several decades: among children, whose sense of community and fair play is allowed to atrophy or is conscientiously discouraged; in universities, where the best and deepest yearnings of students go unacknowledged or untapped; even in literature, where, with very few exceptions, the capacities for generosity and concern which abound unrecognized in most men and women have gone unexamined. But for this to happen to the vets is perhaps the greatest waste of all, since, in many of them, so much understanding has so obviously emerged from their experience.

It takes time for psychic wounds to heal.

What astonishes me is that this situation is being ignored by the American intellectual community, even by those whose resistance to the war was based on moral principles and doubts. The quandaries of the vets, and their pain—a pain they bear for the rest of the nation that now refuses to confront it—certainly demand the attention of intelligent men and women. And their quandaries and pain also provide the best subject I know—the most real, the most immediate—for the kind of moral speculation and self-investigation one would have expected to see in the wake of the war.

But most of the intellectuals concerned with the war have largely ignored the vets; Robert Jay Lifton and Gloria Emerson are the only intellectuals I know who have made the effort to contact them directly and help them think through their condition. And effort is what is takes, because the lines between American castes are so clearly drawn, and our acquiescence to them so nearly complete, that there is no natural way for vets and intellectuals to come together. There is, in effect, a set of social pass-book laws at work—not overt, of course, but implicit, so deeply internal-bred and so much taken for granted that we never notice it.

Friends tell me that the vets are probably better off because of this, since most intellectuals are so limited in understanding and generosity. Perhaps that is true; it may well be that the intellectuals I am talking about exist only in my mind. Still, as limited as the intellectual world may be, there are people within it whose intelligence and understanding of moral issues would, if coupled with generosity and compassion, be of immense use to the vets. Robert Coles is one, for instance, and Arthur Miller, John Seeley and I. F. Stone are others. A few hours with any one of these men might save some vets months and months of agonizing.

The fact that such contacts are not often made results in a double loss. The first loss is to the vets themselves. I often find myself telling them that they are not likely to find anywhere the kinds of help they want or need, and that whatever moral wisdom America gains from the war will result from their efforts and theirs alone. But the fact that I tell them they must do it on their own does not mean that I believe they will be able to do it. Without someone to listen to them, many vets may not accept their right or responsibility to speak openly about moral questions.

Gloria Emerson points out that the vets are hampered in this regard as much by their sense of class as by anything else, and she is probably right. Most vets went into the Army right out of high school and were not the kids who would have gone to college—not the "good" colleges, anyway. They were taught by American institutions to remain mute, to refrain from turning into words what they know or feel. They have, still, in relation to "experts" and intellectuals and academics the odd combination of disdain and exaggerated awe that they had in the Army in relation to authority. They were schooled systematically to doubt the authenticity of their own perceptions and sensibilities; they do not think they have the right to speak; they do not know the tricks of the intellectuals and public trades; and they do not think that what they say will make much difference.

Most important, the vets lack, because they cannot reach those who might provide it, a context for what they feel. They have little sense of the ways in which their suffering is like the suffering of others, so they feel more separated and idiosyncratic than they really are. What many of the vets felt when they returned from Vietnam, for instance, was different in intensity but not in kind from what many returning Peace Corps workers felt: both found the surface of American life surrealistically absurd, somehow less than fully human, not worthy of the seriousness they knew within themselves. And much of what the vets suffer is attendant to all those who live on the margins of society, free of its dominant myths; and this, after all, is something about which some writers and artists know.

Beyond that, most of the vets, though confronted by the deepest philosophical questions, have little knowledge of philosophy or of the great and grave human texts in which over centuries other men and women have created a tradition of concern. The greatest thinkers about guilt, for instance, have been theologians and novelists. Sophocles, Kierkegaard, Conrad in *The Heart of Darkness*, Dostoyevsky in *Crime and Punishment* and Tolstoy in *War and Peace* have all placed at the very heart of human existence the issues that plague the vets.

The vets' suffering, in sum, has in fact brought them closer to the heart of their culture than anything else might have done, but how can they know that, and, knowing, how can they make use of it? For most of them, the deep seriousness visited upon them, which ought to make them feel more fully human, has merely served to isolate them and to make them feel like monsters and pariahs rather than men.

The other losers are the intellectuals themselves, because much of what the vets have to say would be of use to those who took the time to listen. What confronts the vets, after all, is the same moral landscape that contronts us all, a set of ambiguities, confusions and inadequacies that run through our culture from top to bottom. I remember once describing to a woman friend, a writer, how it was the vets felt. "But that's it, that's it exactly," she said. "That's how I felt having my abortions, after the abortions. The same sense of significance and meaning. The same sense of isolation—no one on either side of the question to understand how I felt. The difficulty in straightening it out in my mind, the loneliness of having no one who would forgive me and also understand my refusal to forgive myself."

Never again...

The vets' difficulty in coming to terms with their own past, coupled with their refusal to put it aside, their stubbornness in clinging to its inchoate power, is not very different from the even more hidden yearnings and sorrows of many Americans about many things—yearnings and sorrows for which we no longer have a usable language, and which no longer form (as they once would have) the center of our conversations about what it means to be human.

What is more, the vets' loss of the myths that ordinarily protect people from the truth has brought them face to face with several problems that beleaguer almost all those who approach value from a secular position: the difficulty of dealing with questions of good and evil in the absence of divine, absolute and binding powers or systems. We have learned by now—or we should have—that humans kill just as easily in God's absence as they do in his name, and that the secularization of value, which people believed a hundred years ago might set them free of ignorance and superstition, leads along its own paths to ignorance and superstition. To be absolutely honest, *none* of us who are secular thinkers have anything more than the tatters of past certainty to offer in regard to establishing and sustaining morality, or increasing kindness in men and women and justice in the world. These questions, which plague the vets, ought to plague every thinking man and woman, and none of us can afford to ignore the vets' experience.

In the end, what we owe the dead (whether our own or the Vietnamese), what we owe the vets and what we owe ourselves is the same thing: the resumption of the recurrent conversation about moral values, the sources and meaning of conscience, and the roots of human generosity, solidarity and community. If the Vietnam memorial manages to remind us that this is what is missing and what must be begun, that is fine. If not, then it will become—no matter how moving or lovely—simply another means by which in the name of memory we destroy the past.

Reprinted from *The Nation*, 235, November 27, 1982©. Permission for reprint: *The Nation Magazine*, Nation Associates, Inc.

Peter Marin has listened to Vietnam veterans, and in listening he has become their impassioned spokesman. He has brought to the forefront questions of blame and guilt which have plagued America's relationship to the Vietnam veteran, placing them in a state which he calls "imposed marginality" in our society. Marin, a writer and educator, was the recipient of a 1980 Guggenheim Foundation grant. He now resides in California.

Dealing With Our Vietnam Experience
Robert O. Muller, President, Vietnam Veterans of America

In November, 1982, the National Memorial to the Vietnam War dead was dedicated in Washington, D.C. The occasion marked the first time that tens of thousands of Vietnam veterans had come together since the war. Activities scheduled during the week brought out many strong emotions, rekindling a sense of brotherhood among the veterans. They had indeed shared an extraordinary experience—one that should not be forgotten, and one that now continues to provide the basis for a strong common bond.

Veterans have begun to serve as the nation's conscience, demanding a sense of remembrance and responsibility for what happened. The veterans are now a catalyst, wherever they live, on farms, in the cities and around the country, helping all of us begin the difficult process of dealing with our Vietnam experience.

Robert Muller is the Executive Director of the Washington, D.C. based Vietnam Veterans of America, Inc. This national membership organization for Vietnam-era veterans is engaged in advocacy work designed to promote the general welfare of Vietnam veterans, their dependents and survivors.

Muller joined the U.S. Marine Corp in 1967 and was later commissioned a second lieutenant. Upon his arrival in Vietnam in 1968, he served as a platoon commander, company commander and advisor to the South Vietnamese Army. In April of 1969, while leading South Vietnamese troops in an assault, Muller sustained a gunshot wound which left him permanently paralyzed from the chest down and confined to a wheelchair.

After a year recuperating in a VA hospital, Muller went back to school to earn his law degree from Hofstra Law School in 1974. Muller is married and has two children.

Chapter II

Living with the Past

Minds Still at War:

Guns
Psychological Scars
Suicide
Pride

"I prayed for survival, but forgot peace-of-mind."

Front Porch Warfare I. Bill fires into his front yard for fun, while his daughter protects her ears from the blast.

Front Porch Warfare II.

Vietnam, Kentucky. A Kentucky farm becomes Vietnam for two veterans who need to let off steam.

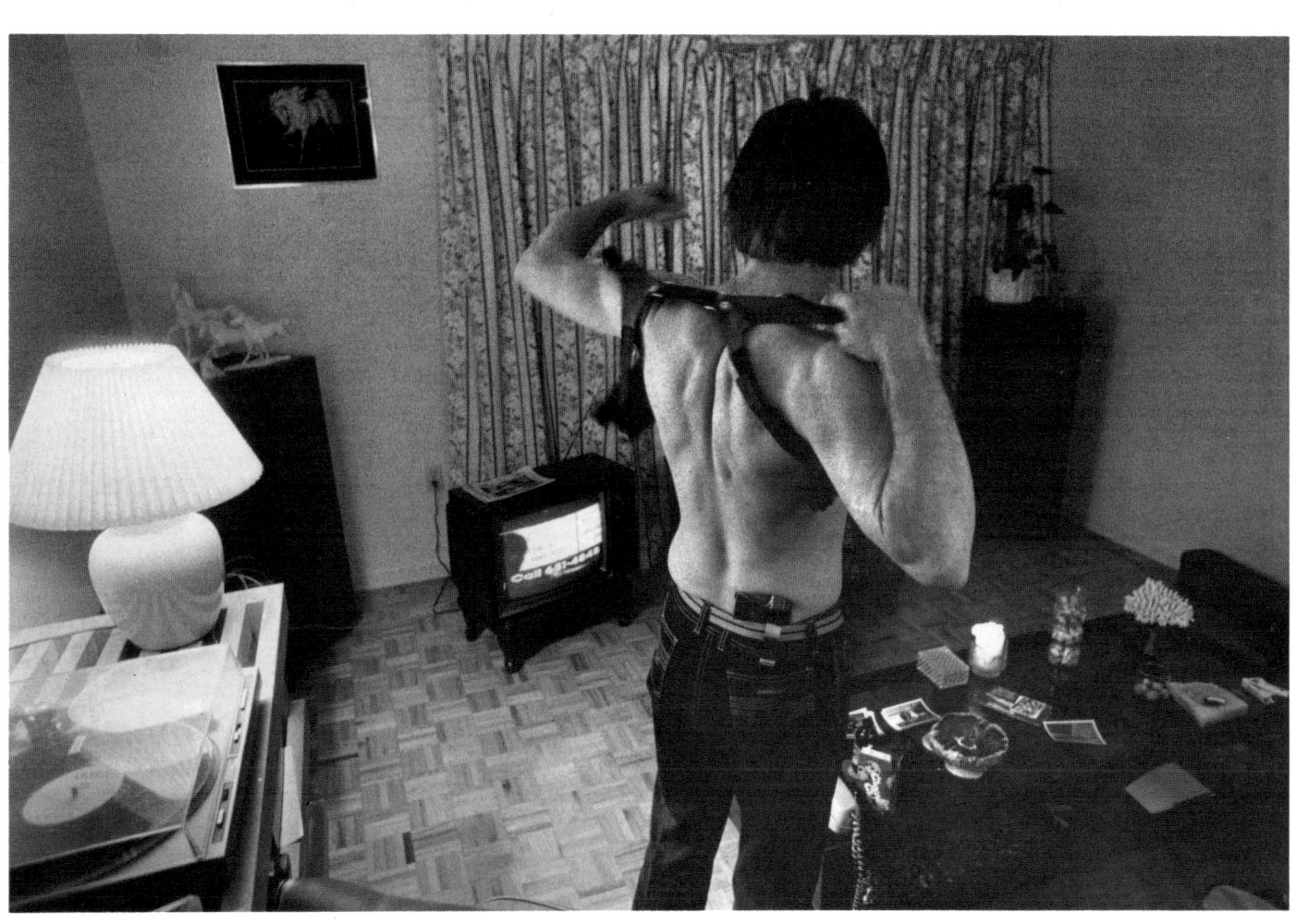

Prisoner of War I. Fully armed in his own home, Paul takes no chances.

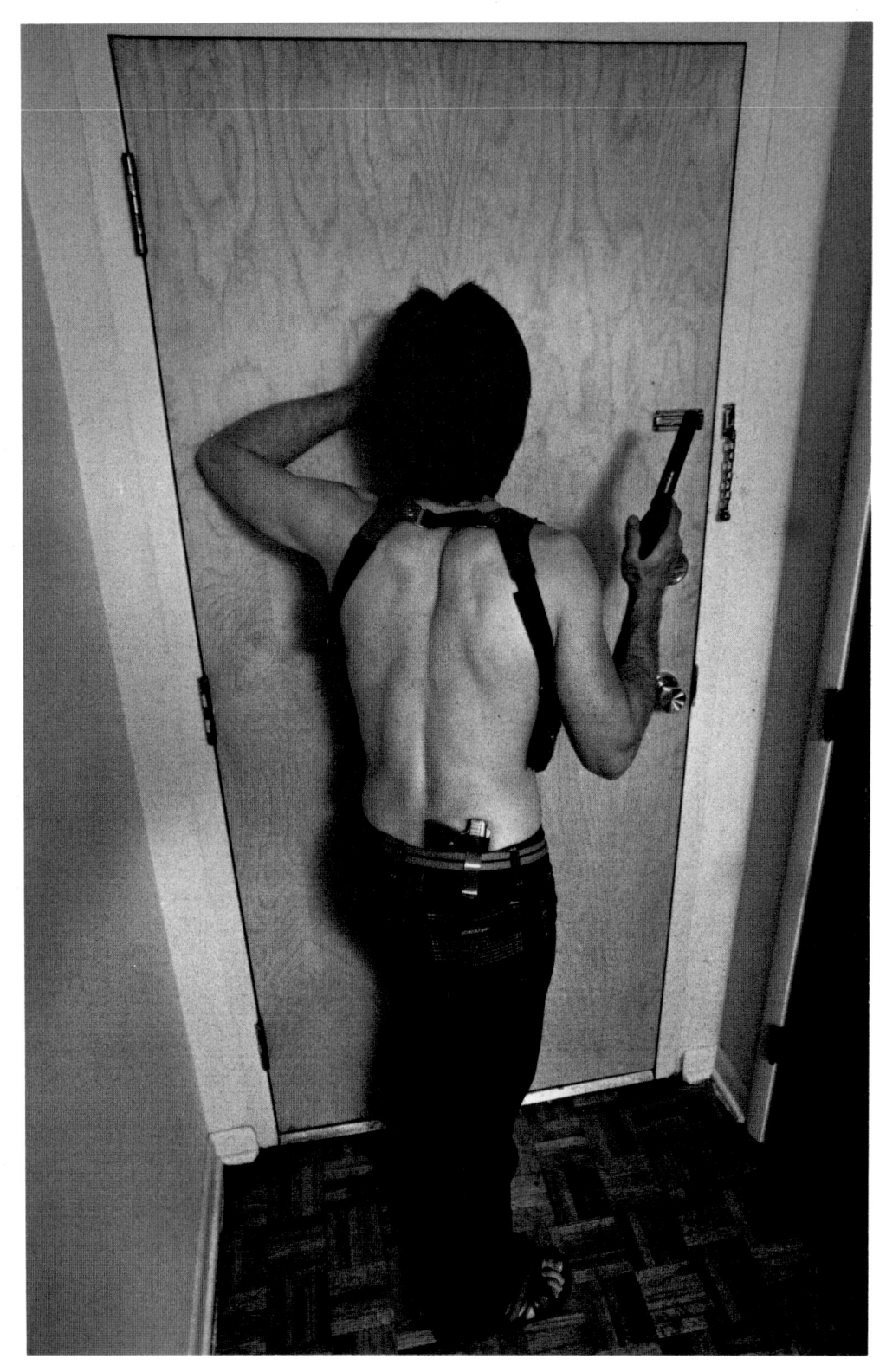

Prisoner of War II. Paul patrols his home, locking all doors and windows against intruders.

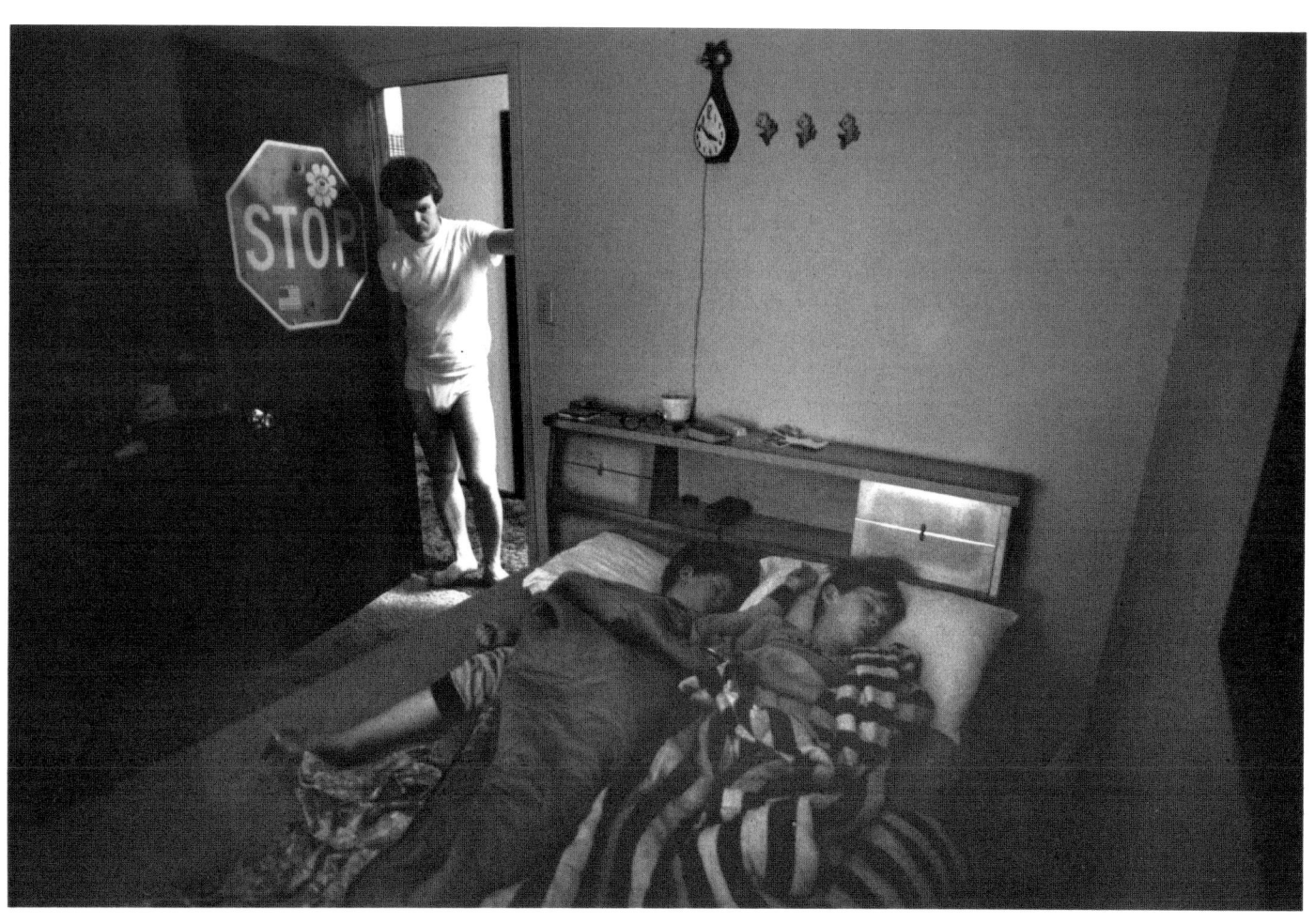

Making Sure...Again. Dennis still suffers sleeplessness, and sometimes checks his children as often as five times a night.

She's Not the Same. Dick reminisces about his marriage prior to the war.

He's Not the Same. Ann tells a Women's Support Group about her husband whom "the war changed so drastically."

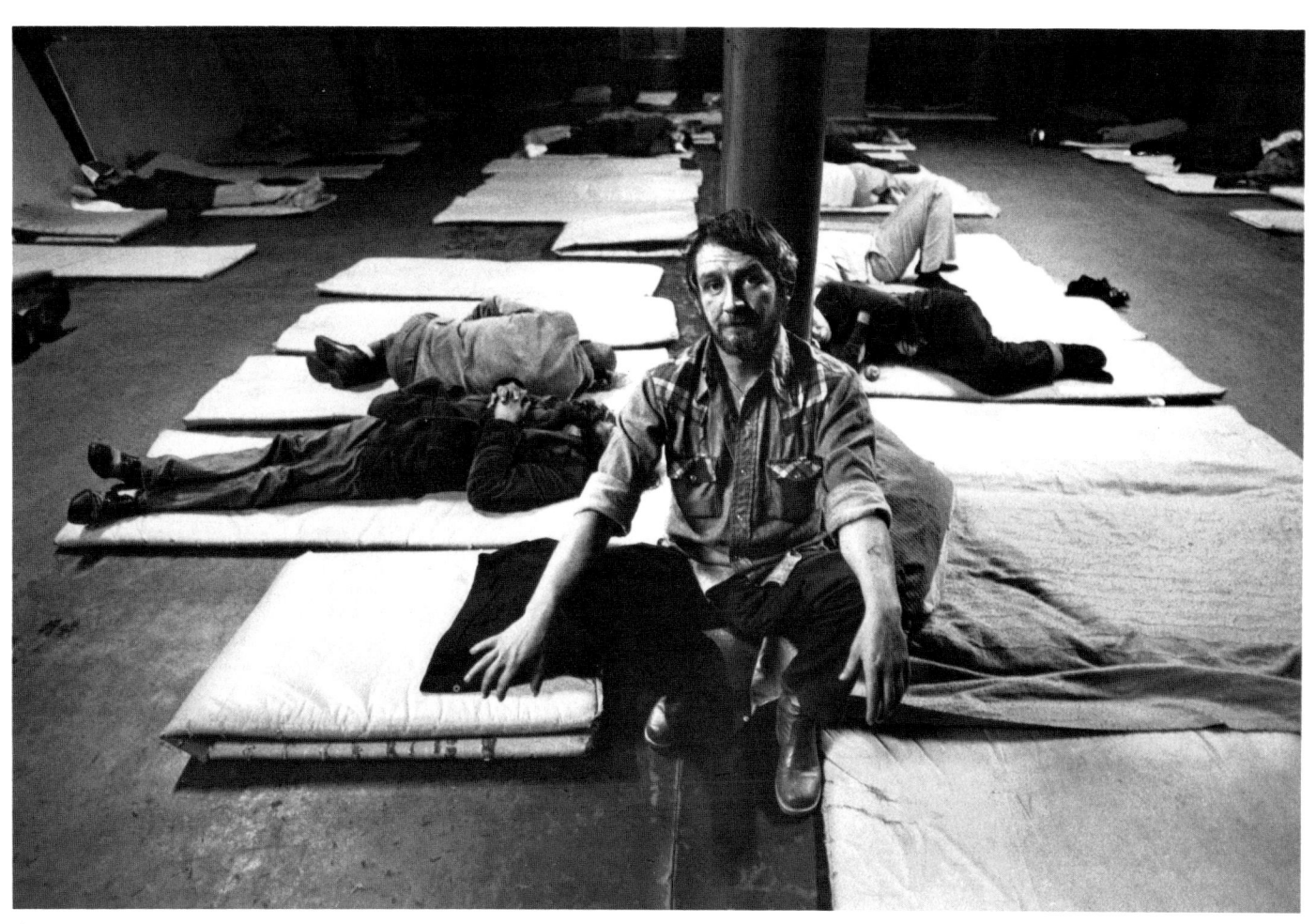

Still Living Close to the Ground. Charlie, a statistic in the high unemployment rate among Vietnam veterans calls the Drop-in Center Home.

Died in Vietnam, Buried Ten Years Later Series. Billy's soul died in Vietnam but his life ended in Kentucky.

Died in Vietnam, Buried Ten Years Later Series. A distraught mother looks for a photograph for her son's casket. She believes he experienced one of his frequent flashbacks, imagining he was walking into a Vietnam jungle. It was a lake and he was drowned.

Billy was her friend.

Chapter III

Families in Transition

Alienation:

The Missing Vet
Unemployment, bankruptcy, over-prescribed drugs

Rejoining the Living

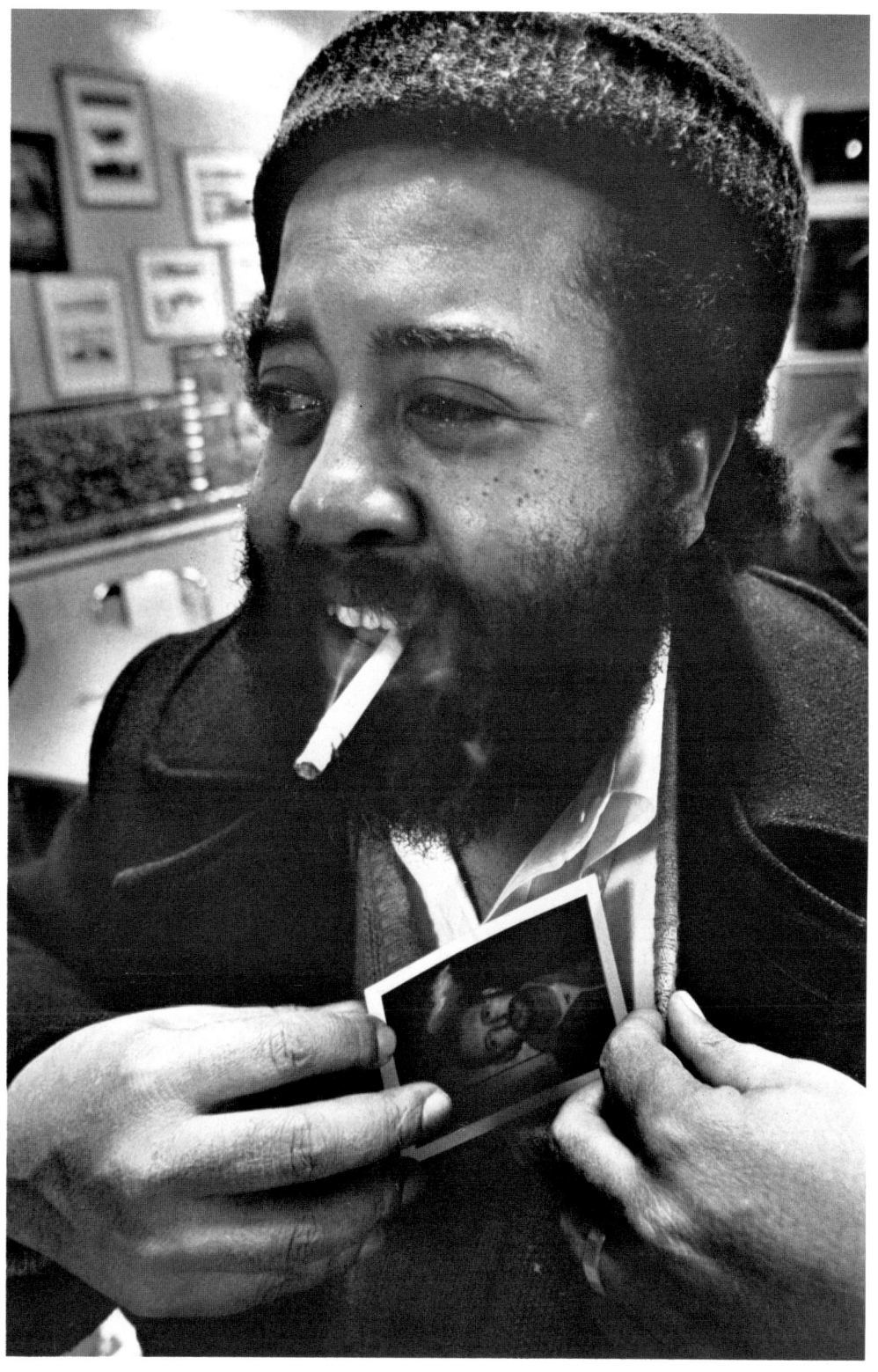

Missing Vet Series. Veteran's Outreach Center counselor, Bernie, begins his search for a missing vet, Bob Watson.

Missing Vet Series.

Missing Vet Series.

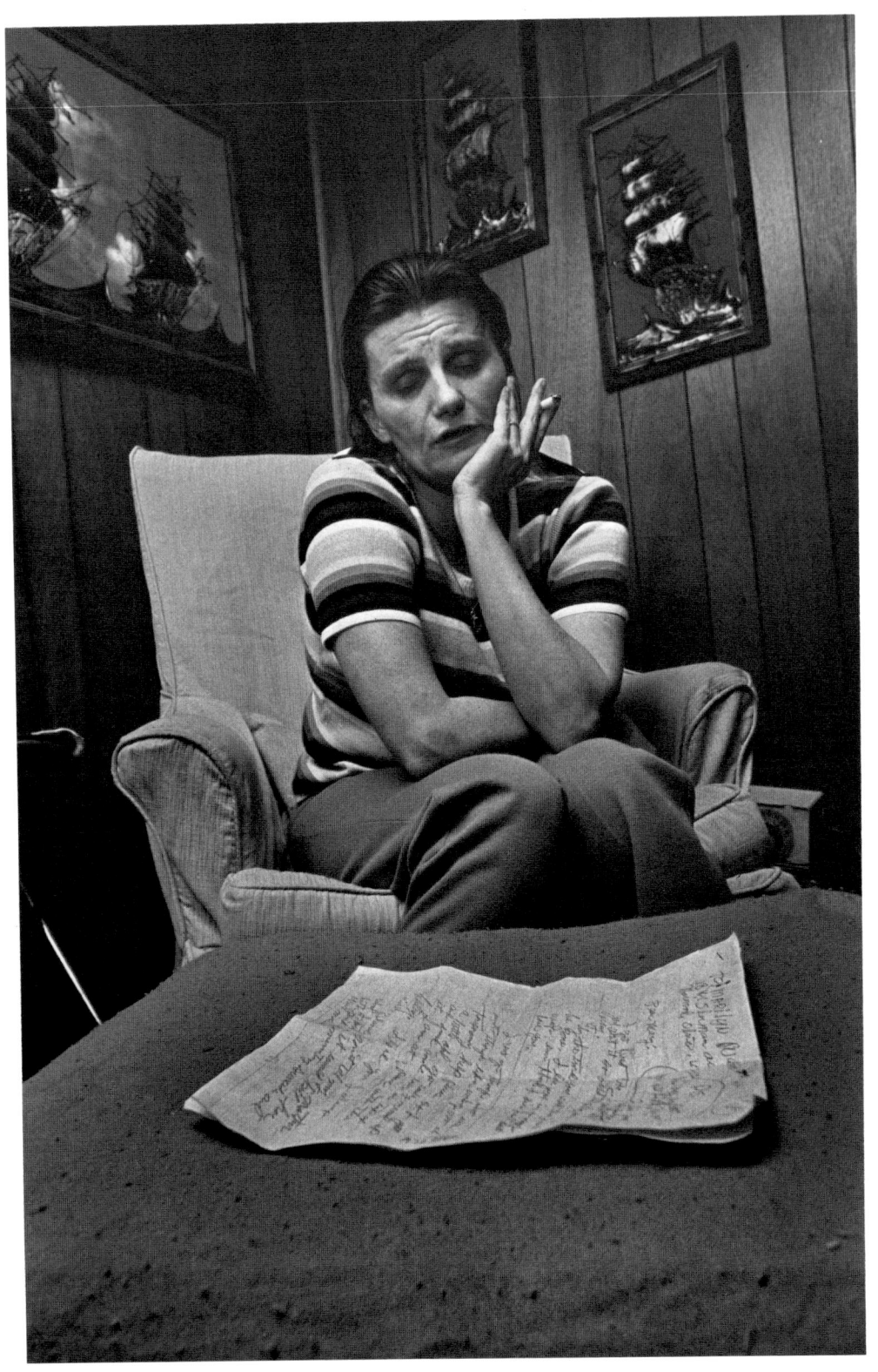

Missing Vet Series. Marilyn Watson stares at a suicide note left by her husband.

Missing Vet Series. Waiting takes its toll on Marilyn Watson.

Jobless and Feeling Useless.

(Mis) Prescription. Drugs have become a part of John's life since he returned from Vietnam.

Things Can Get Better.

Chapter IV

Facing the Problems

Finding Help

Outreach Centers for Vietnam Veterans:

Therapy Sessions
Women's Support Groups

Other Agencies:

Employment Counselling
Test for Agent Orange
Drop-in Centers for Homeless
Building Awareness in the Community

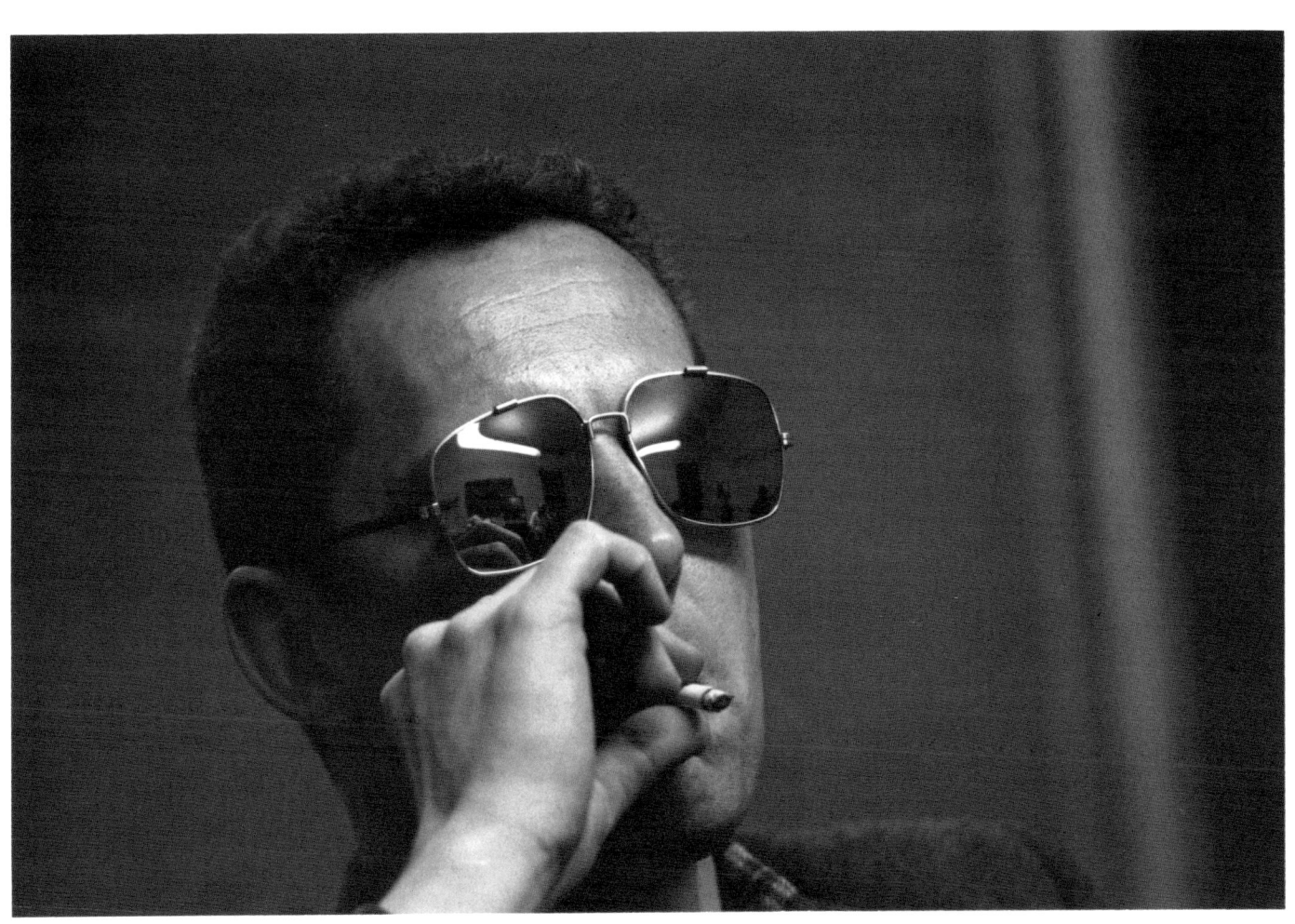

Not Ready Yet. Some vets find it difficult to accept help.

Remembering In Order To Forget. Vets are experiencing past pain in order to live in the present.

Counselor Kean. Bob Kean, leader of a Vietnam Veterans Outreach Center, pauses during a group therapy session.

A women's support group meets weekly at the Cincinnati Outreach Center.

Trio of Veterans. Victims of the war at home, a Women's Support Group meets weekly at the Cincinnati Outreach Center.

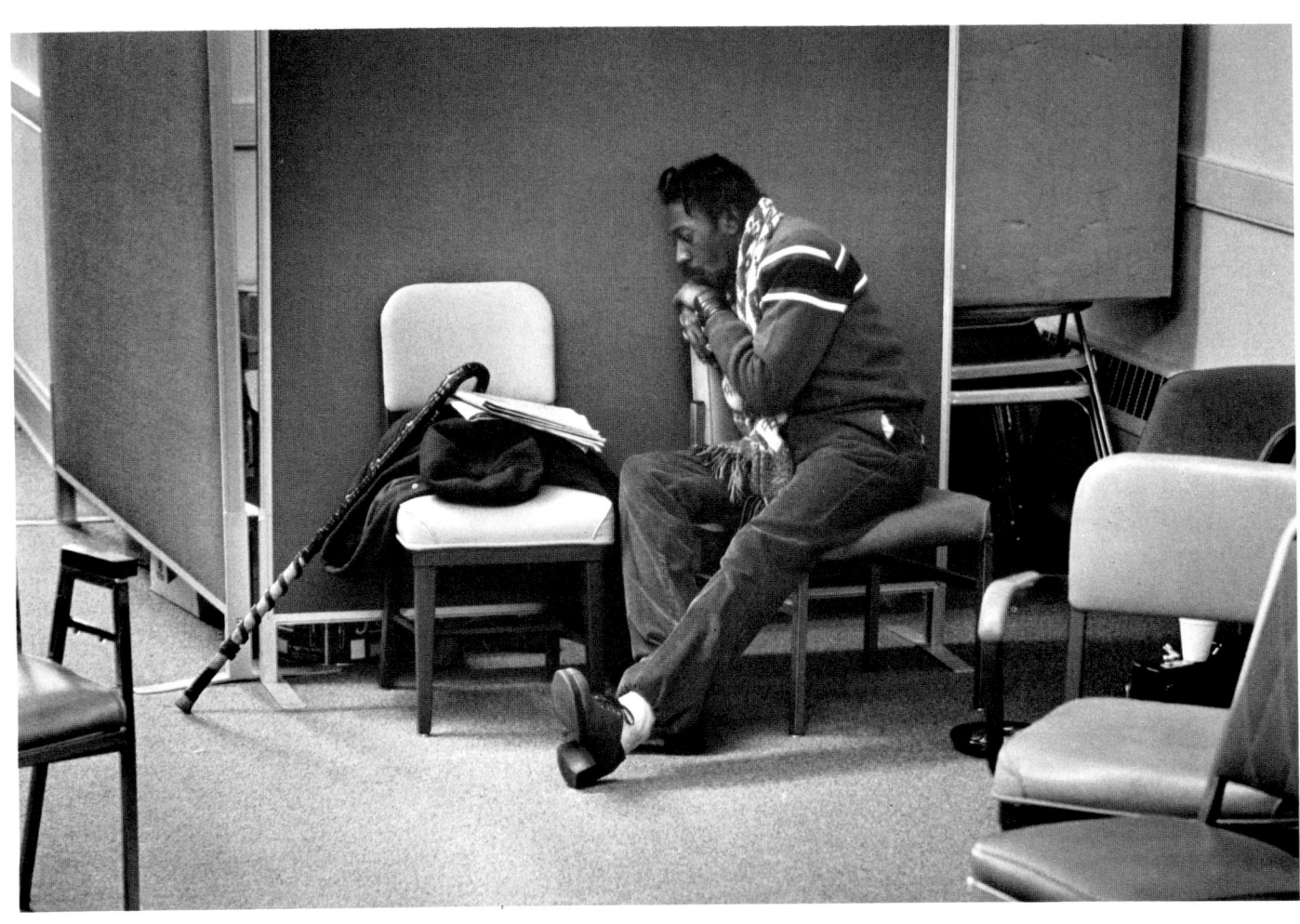

Help Unwanted. Jobless... Charlie has been unable to find work for the past 18 months.

"Do you see any openings in the next ten years?". Vocational testing proves useless to another veteran applying for work.

It Takes Time for Psychic Wounds to Heal.

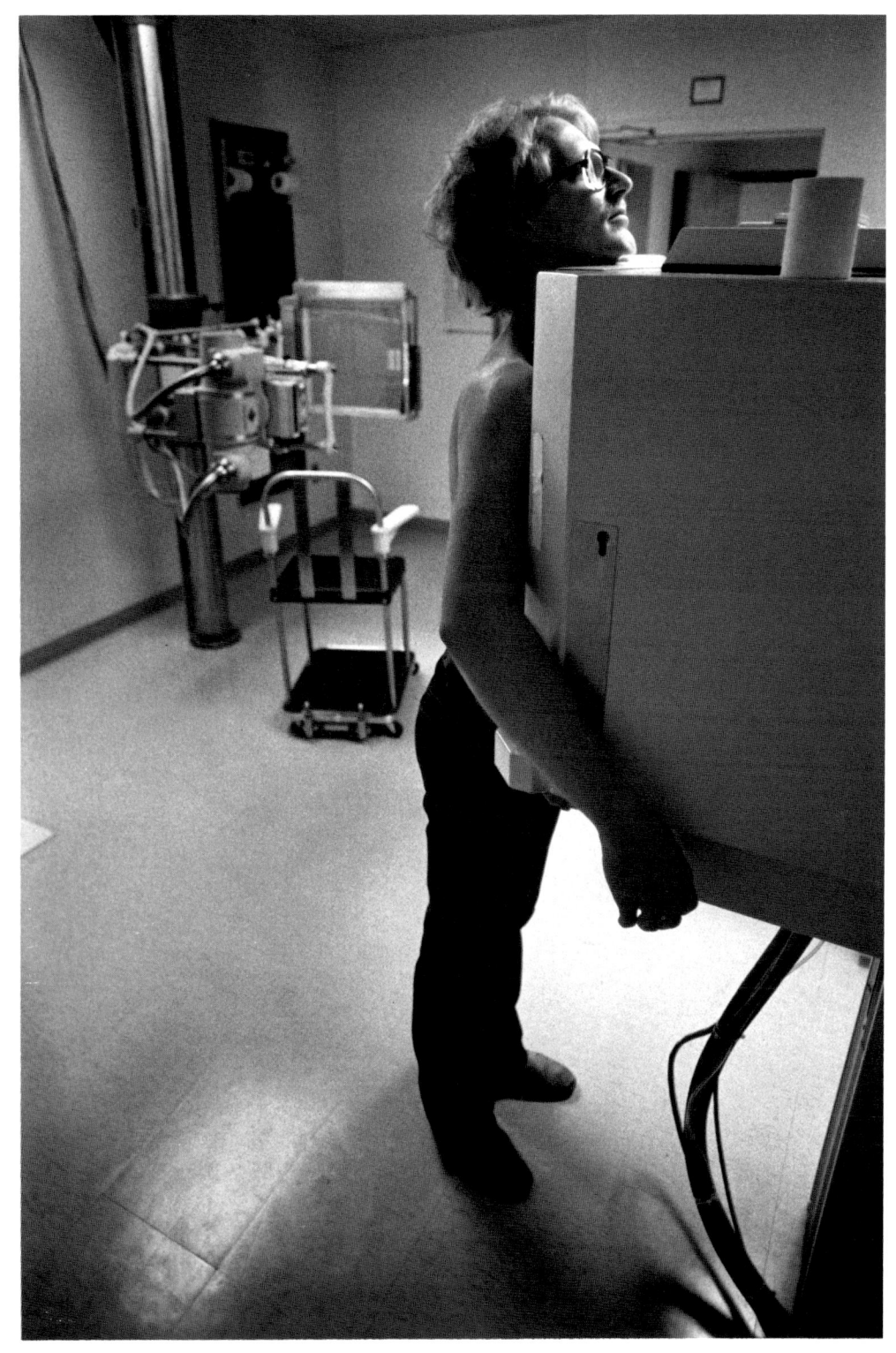

Agent Red, White and Orange. Gary tolerates yet another test.

Building-up, Not Tearing Apart. Bob finds a healthy outlet for his post-Vietnam anger and frustration.

"Silence doesn't work!". Jim discovers sharing his experiences in a group therapy session works for him.

Politicians finally hear the veterans' plight.

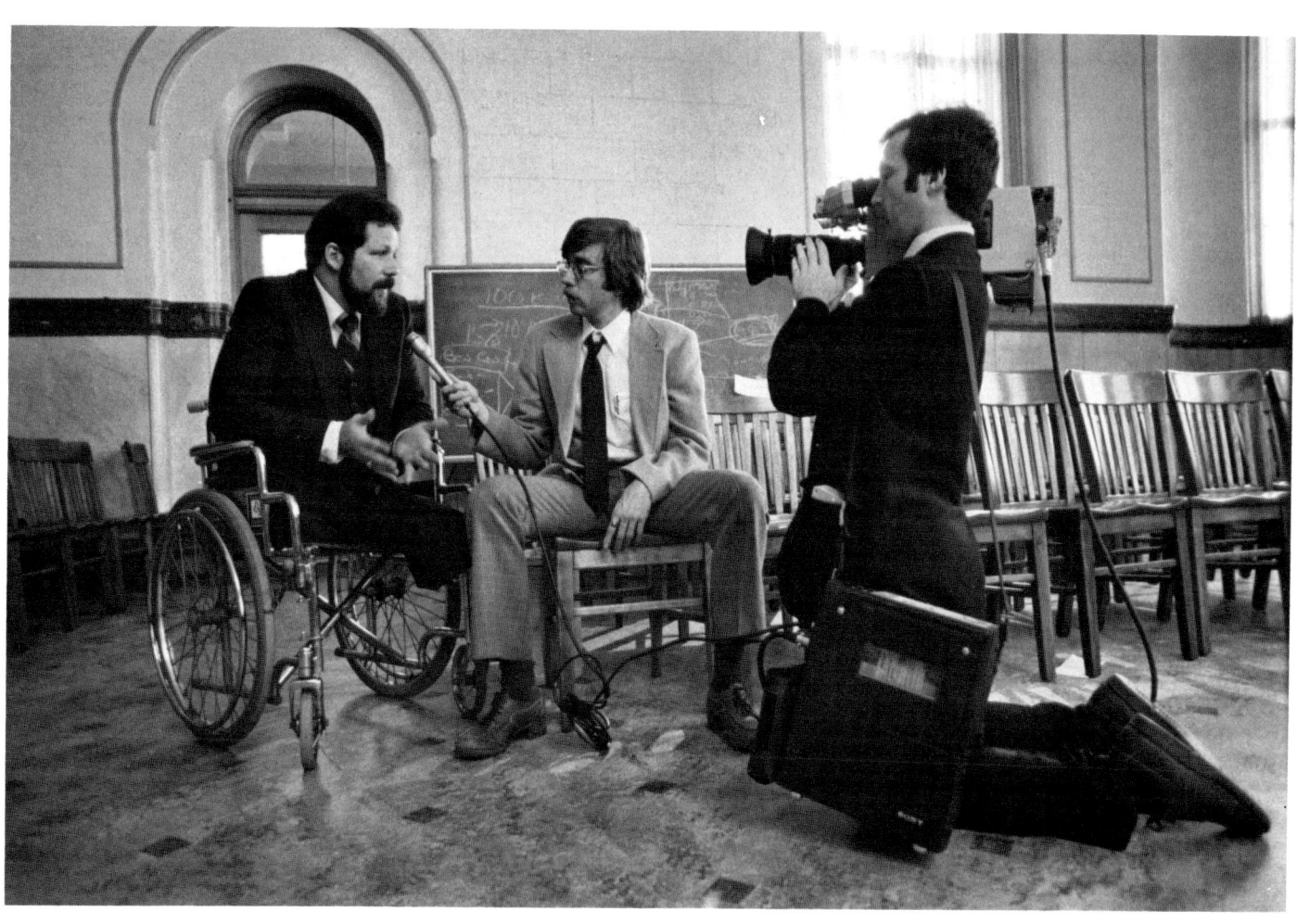

The Nation Begins to Listen. After years of silence, veterans begin to make their voices heard.

VA . . . . friendlies?. A group of vets turn their eyes toward the Cincinnati Veterans Hospital from outside its gates.

Chapter V

The Price

Hunger Strike, Washington, D.C.:

Another Denial

Memorial Dedication, Washington, D.C.:

Reunion
"Welcome Home Vets"
Grieving Parents
The Monument Dedication

Hunger Strike, Washington, D.C. Series. Hoping for understanding.

Hunger Strike, Washington, D.C. Series. The unity of pride.

Hunger Strike, Washington, D.C. Series. The most decorated vet lends his support to hunger strikers.

Hunger Strike, Washington, D.C. Series. Everyday hunger was measured by the display of empty water bottles.

We Understand?, Memorial Dedication, Washington, D.C., Veterans Day, 1982.

Welcome Home I. Memorial Dedication Parade, Washington, D.C., Veterans Day, 1982.

Welcome Home II. Memorial Dedication Parade, Washington, D.C., Veterans Day, 1982.

Universal Braille. Memorial Dedication, Washington, D.C., Veterans Day, 1982.

Veterans Allegory. Memorial Dedication, Washington, D.C., Veterans Day, 1982.

The Fallen Soldier. Memorial Dedication, Washington, D.C., Veterans Day, 1982.

With Roses At Their Feet. Memorial Dedication, Washington, D.C., Veterans Day, 1982.

"A piece of cloth with colors, patterns or devices used as symbol of a nation, organization, etc."[1]
Memorial Dedication, Washington, D.C., Veterans Day, 1982.

[1]Websters New World Dictionary of the American Language. Nashville, Tennessee: The Southwestern Co., 1965.

Outreach Program Directory
V.A. Office
Washington, D.C.
Ray Scoffield
202-393-4120 — 202-389-3059

Alabama, Birmingham
Vet Center
2145 Highland Avenue, Suite 250
Birmingham, AL 35205
205/933-0500

Alabama, Mobile
Vet Center
110 Marine Street
Mobile, AL 36604
205/694-4194

Alaska, Anchorage
Vet Center
550 West 8th Avenue, Room 101
Anchorage, AK 99501
907/277-1501

Alaska, Fairbanks
Vet Center Satellite
515 7th Avenue, Room 230
Fairbanks, AK 99701
907/456-4238

Alaska, Kenai
Vet Center Satellite
905 Cook Street, P.O. Box 1883
Kenai, AK 99611
907/283-5205

Alaska, Wasilla
Vet Center Satellite
Box 957 Mile ½ Knik Road
Wasilla, AK 99687
907/376-4318

Arizona, Phoenix
Vet Center
807 North 3rd Street
Phoenix, AZ 85004
602/261-4769

Arizona, Tucson
Vet Center
727 North Swan
Tucson, AZ 85711
602/323-3271

Arkansas, Little Rock
Vet Center
1311 West 2nd Street
Little Rock, AR 72201
501/378-6395

California, Anaheim
Vet Center
859 South Harbor Blvd.
Anaheim, CA 92805
714/776-0161

California, Concord
Vet Center
1899 Clayton Road, Suite 140
Concord, CA 94520
415/680-4529

California, Fresno
Vet Center
1340 Van Ness Avenue
Fresno, CA 93721
209/487-5660

California, Los Angeles
Vet Center
251 West 85th Place
Los Angeles, CA 90003
213/753-1391

California, Los Angeles
Vet Center
2000 Westwood Blvd.
Los Angeles, CA 90025
213/475-9509

California, Montabello
Vet Center
2449 West Beverly Blvd.
Montabello, CA 90640
213/728-9984—9999

California, Northridge
Vet Center
18924 Roscoe Blvd.
Northridge, CA 91335
213/993-8862

California, Oakland
Vet Center
616 16th Street
Oakland, CA 94612
415/763-3904

California, Riverside
Vet Center
4954 Arlington Avenue
Riverside, CA 92504
714/359-8967

California, San Diego
Vet Center
2900 6th Avenue
San Diego, CA 92103
619/294-2040

California, San Francisco
Vet Center
1708 Waller Street
San Francisco, CA 94117
415/386-6726—6727

California, San Francisco
Vet Center
2989 Mission Street
San Francisco, CA 94110
415/824-5111—2141

California, San Jose
Vet Center
1648 West Santa Clara Street
San Jose, CA 95116
408/258-5600—5514

California, San Jose
Vet Center
361 S. Monroe Street, Suite 605
San Jose, CA 95128
408/249-1643—1677

Colorado, Colorado Springs
Vet Center Satellite
875 West Moreno Avenue
Colorado Springs, CO 80905
303/633-2902

Colorado, Denver
Vet Center
1820 Gilpin Street
Denver, CO 80218
303/861-9281—7521

Connecticut, Hartford
Vet Center
370 Market Street
Hartford, CT 06510
203/244-3543—3544

Connecticut, New Haven
Vet Center
562 Whalley Avenue
New Haven, CT 06510
203/773-2235—2246

Delaware, Wilmington
Vet Center
Van Buren Medical Center
1411 N. Van Buren Street
Wilmington, DE 19806
302/571-8277

District of Columbia, Washington
Vet Center
709 8th Street, S.E.
Washington, DC 20003
202/745-8400—8401

Florida, Ft. Lauderdale
Vet Center
400 E. Prospect Road
Ft. Lauderdale, FL 3334
305/563-2992—2993

Florida, Jacksonville
Vet Center
255 Liberty Street
Jacksonville, FL 32202
904/791-3621

Florida, Miami
Vet Center
2615 Biscayne Blvd.
Miami, FL 33137
305/573-8830—8831

Florida, Orlando
Vet Center
333 North Orange
Orlando, FL 32801
305/420-6151—6152

Florida, St. Petersburg
Vet Center
235 31st Street, North
St. Petersburg, FL 33713
813/327-3355

Florida, Tampa
Vet Center
1507 W. Sligh Avenue
Tampa, FL 33604
813/228-2621

Georgia, Atlanta
Vet Center
65 11th Street, N.E.
Atlanta, GA 30309
404/881-7264

Hawaii, Honolulu
Vet Center
1370 Kapiolani Blvd., Suite 201
Honolulu, HI 96814
808/546-3743—3723

Idaho, Boise
Vet Center
103 West State Street
Boise, ID 83702
208/342-3612

Illinois, Chicago
Vet Center
547 West Roosevelt Road
Chicago, IL 60607
312/829-4400—4401

Illinois, Chicago Heights
Vet Center
1600 Halsted Street
Chicago Heights, IL 60411
312/754-0340

Illinois, Oak Park
Vet Center
155 South Oak Park Avenue
Oak Park, IL 60302
312/383-3225—3226

Illinois, Peoria
Vet Center
605 N.E. Monroe
Peoria, IL 61603
309/671-7300

Indiana, Evansville
Vet Center
101 N. Kentucky Avenue
Evansville, IN 47711
812/425-0311

Indiana, Fort Wayne
Vet Center
528 West Berry Street
Fort Wayne, IN 46802
219/423-9456—9457

Indiana, Indianapolis
Vet Center
811 Massachusetts Avenue
Indianapolis, IN 46204
317/269-2838

Iowa, Des Moines
Vet Center
3619 6th Avnue
Des Moines, IA 50313
515/284-6119—6120

Iowa, Sioux City
Vet Center Satellite
706 Jackson
Sioux City, IA 51101
712/233-3200

Kansas, Wichita
Vet Center
310 South Laura
Wichita, KS 67211
316/265-3260

Kentucky, Lexington
Vet Center
249 West Short Street
Lexington, KY 40507
606/231-8387

Kentucky, Louisville
Vet Center
736 South 1st Street
Louisville, KY 40202
502/589-1981

Louisiana, New Orleans
Vet Center
1529 N. Claiborne Avenue
New Orleans, LA 70116
504/943-8386

Maine, Bangor
Vet Center
96 Harlow Street
Bangor, ME 04401
207/947-3391—3392

Maine, Portland
Vet Center
175 Lancaster Street, Room 213
Portland, ME 04101
207/780-3584—3585

Maryland, Baltimore
Vet Center
1420 W. Patapsco Avenue, Patapsco Plaza
Baltimore, MD 21230
301/355-8592

Maryland, Baltimore
Vet Center
Mondawmin Shopping Ctr.
1153 Mondawmin Concourse
Baltimore, MD 21215
301/728-8924

Maryland, Elkton
Vet Center
7 Elkton Commercial Plaza
Elkton, MD 21921
301/398-0171

Maryland, Silver Spring
Vet Center
8121 Georgia Avenue, Suite 500
Silver Spring, MD 20910
202/745-8210—8396

Massachusetts, Boston
Vet Center
480 Tremont Street
Boston, MA 02116
617/451-0171—0172

Massachusetts, Brighton
Vet Center
71 Washington Street
Brighton, MA 02135
617/782-1032—1013

Massachusetts, Brockton
Vet Center
15 Bolton Place
Brockton, MA 02401
617/580-2730—2731

Massachusetts, Springfield
Vet Center
1985 Main Street, Northgate Plaza
Springfield, MA 01103
413/737-5167

Michigan, Detroit
Vet Center
18411 West Seven Mile Road
Detroit, MI 48219
313/535-3333—3334

Michigan, Grand Rapids
Vet Center
1940 Eastern Avenue S.E.
Grand Rapids, MI 49507
616/243-0385

Michigan, Southgate
Vet Center
14405 North Line
Southgate, MI 48195
313/282-9852—9853

Minnesota, St. Paul
Vet Center
2480 University Avenue
St. Paul, MN 55114
612/644-4022—5601

Mississippi, Jackson
Vet Center
158 E. Pascagoula Street
Jackson, MS 39201
601/353-4912

Missouri, Kansas City
Vet Center
3600 Broadway, Suite 19
Kansas City, MO 64111
816/753-1866—2075

Missouri, St. Louis
Vet Center
2345 Pine Street
St. Louis, MO 63103
314/231-1260

Montana, Billings
Vet Center
415 North 33rd Street
Billings, MT 59101
406/657-6071

Nebraska, Lincoln
Vet Center
1240 North 10th Street
Lincoln, NE 68508
402/476-9736

Nebraska, Omaha
Vet Center
5123 Leavenworth Street
Omaha, NE 68106
402/553-2068

Nevada, Las Vegas
Vet Center
214 South 8th Street
Las Vegas, NV 89101
702/385-6368—6369

Nevada, Reno
Vet Center
341 South Arlington Street
Reno, NV 89501
702/323-1294

New Hampshire, Manchester
Vet Center
14 Pearl Street
Manchester, NH 03104
603/668-7060—7061

New Jersey, Jersey City
Vet Center
626 Newark Avenue
Jersey City, NJ 07306
201/656-6986

New Jersey, Newark
Vet Center
1030 Broad Street
Newark, NJ 07102
201/622-6941

New Jersey, Trenton
Vet Center
318 East State Street
Trenton, NJ 08608
609/989-2260—2261

New Mexico, Albuquerque
Vet Center
4603 4th Street, N.W.
Albuquerque, NM 87107
505/345-8366—8876

New Mexico, Gallup
Vet Center Satellite
211 West Mesa
Gallup, NM 87301
505-722-3821—3822

New York, Albany
Vet Center
875 Central Avenue, West Mall Office Plaza
Albany, NY 12208
518/438-2508

New York, Babylon
Vet Center
116 West Main Street
Babylon, NY 11702
516/661-3930

New York, Bronx
Vet Center
226 East Fordham Road, Rooms 216/217
Bronx, NY 10458
212/367-3500—3501

New York, Brooklyn
Vet Center
165 Cadman Plaza, East
Brooklyn, NY 11201
212/330-2825—2826

New York, Buffalo
Vet Center
114 Elmwood Avenue
Buffalo, NY 14201
716/882-0505

New York, Jamaica Hills
Vet Center
148-43 Hillside Avenue
Jamaica Hills, NY 11435
212/658-6767—6768

New York, Manhattan
Vet Center
166 West 75th Street
Manhattan, NY 10023
212/944-2917—2930

New York, White Plains
Vet Center Satellite
200 Hamilton Avenue, White Plains Mall
White Plains, NY 10601
914/684-0570

North Carolina, Charlotte
Vet Center
910 North Alexander Street, Suite 210
Charlotte, NC 28206
704/333-6107—6108

North Carolina, Fayetteville
Vet Center
4 Market Square
Fayetteville, NC 28301
919/323-4908

North Dakota, Fargo
Vet Center
1322 Gateway Drive
Fargo, ND 58103
701/237-0942

North Dakota, Minot
Vet Center
108 Burdick Expressway
Minot, ND 58701
701/852-0177

Ohio, Cincinnati
Vet Center
31 East 12th Street, 4th Floor
Cincinnati, OH 45202
513/241-9420—9421

Ohio, Cleveland
Vet Center
10605 Carnegie Avenue
Cleveland, OH 44106
216/791-9224—7495

Ohio, Cleveland
Vet Center
11511 Lorain Avenue
Cleveland, OH 44111
216/671-8530—8531

Ohio, Columbus
Vet Center
1751 Cleveland Avenue
Columbus, OH 43211
614/291-2227

Ohio, Dayton
Vet Center
438 Wayne Avenue
Dayton, OH 45410
513/461-9150—9151

Oklahoma, Oklahoma City
Vet Center
4111 North Lincoln Blvd. #10
Oklahoma City, OK 73105
405/521-9308

Oklahoma, Tulsa
Vet Center
1605 South Boulder
Tulsa, OK 74119
918/581-7105

Oregon, Eugene
Vet Center
1247 Villard
Eugene, OR 97403
503/687-6918

Oregon, Portland
Vet Center
2450 S.E. Belmont
Portland, OR 97214
503/231-1586

Pennsylvania, Harrisburg
Vet Center
127 State Street
Harrisburg, PA 17101
717/782-3954

Pennsylvania, Monroeville
Vet Center Satellite
4328 Old William Penn Highway
Monroeville, PA 15146
412/372-8627—8628

Pennsylvania, Philadelphia
Vet Center
1107 Arch Street
Philadelphia, PA 19107
215/627-0238

Pennsylvania, Philadelphia
Vet Center
5601 North Broad Street, Room 202
Philadelphia, PA 19141
215/924-4670

Pennsylvania, Pittsburgh
Vet Center
954 Penn Avenue
Pittsburgh, PA 15222
412/765-1193

Puerto Rico, Rio Piedras
Vet Center
Suite LC-8A/9 Medical Center Plaza
La Riviera
Rio Piedras, RQ 00921
809/783-8269

Puerto Rico, St. Croix
Vet Center Satellite
St. Croix, RQ 00921

Puerto Rico, St. Thomas
Vet Center
Havensight Mall (116V)
St. Thomas, RQ 00802
809/774-6674

Rhode Island, Pawtucket
Vet Center
172 Pine Street
Pawtucket, RI 02860
401/728-9501—9502

South Carolina, Greenville
Vet Center
904 Pendleton Street
Greenville, SC 29601
803/271-2711

South Carolina, No. Charleston
Vet Center
3366 Rivers Avenue
No. Charleston, SC 29405
803/747-8387

South Dakota, Rapid City
Vet Center
610 Kansas City Street
Rapid City, SD 57701
605/348-0077

South Dakota, Sioux Falls
Vet Center
100 West 6th Street, Suite 101
Sioux Falls, SD 57102
605/332-0856

Tennessee, Knoxville
Vet Center
1515 E. Magnolia Avenue, Suite 201
Knoxville, TN 37917
615/971-5866

Tennessee, Memphis
Vet Center
1 North 3rd Street
Memphis, TN 38103
901/521-3506

Texas, Dallas
Vet Center
5415 Maple Plaza, Suite 114
Dallas, TX 75235
214/634-7024

Texas, El Paso
Vet Center
2121 Wyoming Street
El Paso, TX 79903
915/542-2851—2852

Texas, Fort Worth
Vet Center
Seminary South Office Building, Suite 10
Fort Worth, TX 76115
817/921-3733

Texas, Houston
Vet Center
4905A San Jacinto Street
Houston, TX 77004
713/522-5354—5376

Texas, Laredo
Vet Center
717 Corpus Christi
Laredo, TX 78040
512/723-4680

Texas, San Antonio
Vet Center
107 Lexington Avenue
San Antonio, TX 78205
512/229-4025

Texas, San Antonio
Vet Center
1916 Fredericksburg Road
San Antonio, TX 78201
512/229-4120

Utah, Salt Lake City
Vet Center
216 East 5th Street South
Salt Lake City, UT 84102
801/584-1294

Vermont, White River Junction
Vet Center
75 Woodstock Road
White River Junction, VT 05001
802/295-2908

Vermont, Williston
Vet Center Satellite
RFD#2, Tafts Corners
Williston, VT 05495
802/878-3371

Virginia, Norfolk
Vet Center
7450 ½ Tidewater Drive
Norfolk, VA 23505
804/587-1338

Virginia, Richmond
Vet Center
Gresham Court Box 83
1030 West Franklin Street
Richmond, VA 23220
804/353-8958

Washington, Seattle
Vet Center
1322 East Pike Street
Seattle, WA 98122
206/442-2706

Washington, Spokane
Vet Center
North 1611 Division
Spokane, WA 99207
509/326-6970—6979

Washington, Tacoma
Vet Center
4801 Pacific Avenue
Tacoma, WA 98408
206/473-0731—0732

West Virginia, Huntington
Vet Center
1014 6th Avenue
Huntington, WV 25701
304/523-8387

West Virginia, Morgantown
Vet Center
1191 Pineview Drive
Morgantown, WV 26505
304/291-4001—4002

Wisconsin, Madison
Vet Center
147 South Butler Street
Madison, WI 53703
608/264-5343

Wisconsin, Milwaukee
Vet Center
3400 Wisconsin
Milwaukee, WI 53208
414/344-5504

Wisconsin, Superior
Vet Center
1225 Tower Avenue, Suite 315
Superior, WI 54880
715/394-2566

Wyoming, Casper
Vet Center Satellite
641 East Second Street
Casper, WY 82601
307/235-8010

Wyoming, Cheyenne
Vet Center
1810 Pioneer Street
Cheyenne, WY 82001
307/778-2660

BIBLIOGRAPHY

Professional Books and Journal Articles

American Psychiatric Association. *Diagnostic and Statistical Manual III. (DSM III)*. Washington, D.C., 1980

Anderson, R. S., ed. *Neuropsychiatry in World War II*. Volume I. Washington, D.C.: Office of the Surgeon General, 1966.

Archibald, H. E. and Tuddenham, R. D. Persistent stress reaction after combat. A twenty year follow-up. *Archives of General Psychiatry* 12:475-481, 1965.

Barry, J. and Ehrhart, W. D., eds. *Demilitarized Zones: Veterans After Vietnam*. Perkasie, Pa: East River Anthology, 1976.

Berman, S., Price, S. and Gusman, F. An inpatient program for Vietnam combat veterans in Veterans Administration Hospital. *Hospital and Community Psychiatry* 33:919-922, 1982.

Bitzer, R. Caught in the middle: mentally disabled veterans and the Veterans Administration in *Strangers At Home: Vietnam Veterans Since the War*. Edited by Figley, C. R., Leventman, S. New York: Praeger Publications, 1980.

Blank, A. S. Jr. Apocalypse terminable and interminable: Operation Outreach for Vietnam veterans. *Hospital and Community Psychiatry* 33:913-918, 1982.

Blank, A. S. Jr., et. al. Army psychiatry in Vietnam, 1965-67: A symposium in *Proceedings of Social and Preventive Psychiatry Course*, 1967. Edited by Jones, F. D. Washington, D.C.: U.S. Government Printing Office, 1980.

Blank, A. S. Jr. Stresses of war: The example of Vietnam in the *Handbook of Stress*. Edited by Goldberger, L., Breznitz, S. New York: Free Press/Macmillan, 1981.

Blank, A. S. Jr. Traditional Veterans Administration psychiatric services in *First Training Conference Papers, Operation Outreach*. Washington, D.C.: Veterans Administration, 1979.

Borus, J. F. Incidence of maladjustment in Vietnam returnees. *Archives of General Psychiatry* 30:554-557, 1974.

Borus, J. F. Reentry: III. Facilitating healthy readjustment in Vietnam veterans. *Psychiatry* 36:428-439, 1973.

Boulanger, G. Changes in stress reactions over time, in *Legacies of Vietnam*, Volume 4: Long-Term Stress Reactions: Some Causes, Consequences and Naturally Occurring Support Systems. Washington, D.C.: Government Printing Office, 1981.

Boulanger, G. Current stress reactions, *ibid*.

Boulanger, G. Family stability and stress reactions, *ibid*.

Boulanger, G. The incidence of stress reactions immediately after the period of greater involvement in the Vietnam era, *ibid*.

Boulanger, G. Who goes to war? *ibid*.

Bourne, P. G. *Men, Stress and Vietnam*. Boston: Little Brown, 1970.

Bourne, P. G. Military psychiatry and the Vietnam experience. *American Journal of Psychiatry* 127:481-488, 1970.

Brill, N. Q. and Beebe, G. W. A follow-up study of war neuroses. *Veterans Administration Medical Monograph*. Washington, D.C.: U.S. Government Printing Office, 1955.

Buttinger, J. *Vietnam: The Unforgettable Tragedy*. New York: Horizon, 1977.

Camacho, P. From war hero to criminal: The negative privilege of the Vietnam veteran, in *Strangers At Home: Vietnam Veterans Since the War*. Edited by Figley, C. R., Leventman, S. New York: Praeger Publications, 1980.

Cleland, Mr. *Strong At the Broken Places*. Lincoln, Va: Chosen Books, 1980.

Dancey, T. E. Treatment in the absence of pensioning for psychoneurotic veterans. *American Journal of Psychiatry* 107:347-349, 1950.

DeFazio, V. J. Dynamic perspectives on the nature and effects of combat stress, in *Stress Disorders Among Vietnam Veterans: Theory, Research and Treatment*. Edited by Figley, C. R. New York: Brunner/Mazel, 1978.

Diagnostic and Statistical Manual, Edition III. Washington, D.C.: American Psychiatric Association, 1980.

DiMascio, A., Shader, R. and Harmatz, J. Psychotropic drugs and induced hostility. *Psychosomatics* 10:47-50, 1969.

Domash, M. and Sparr, L. F. Post-traumatic stress disorder masquerading as paranoid schizophrenia. *Military Medicine* (in press).

Egendorf, A. Human development and ultimate reality: The perceptual grounds for transformation, in *Dimensions of Thought: Current Explorations in Time, Space and Knowledge*, Volume 2. Edited by Tulku, T., Moon, R., Randall, G.S. Berkeley, California: Dharma Press, 1980.

Egendorf, A. et. al. *Legacies of Vietnam: Comparative Adjustment of Veteran and Their Peers*. Washington, D.C.: U.S. Government Printing Office, 1981.

Egendorf, A. One Vietnam veteran: A study of continuity and change. *Dissertation Abstracts International* 38(4):1877-8B, 1978.

Egendorf, A. Psychotherapy with Vietnam veterans, in *Stress Reactions After Vietnam: Theory and Research*. Edited by Figley, C. F. New York: Brunnel/Mazel, 1978.

Egendorf, A. Statement on behalf of the Association for the Advancement of Psychology and the American Psychological Association, in *Hearings of the Committee on Veterans Affairs*, U.S. Senate, 96th Congress, May 21, 1980. Washington, D.C.: U.S. Government Printing Office, 1980.

Egendorf, A. The postwar healing of Vietnam veterans: Recent research. *Hospital and Community Psychiatry* 33(11):901-908, November 1982.

Egendorf, A. Veterans and the legacy of Vietnam, in *The Psychology of Being Human*, Brief Update Edition by Rubin, Z., McNeil, E. G. New York: Harper & Row, 1982.

Egendorf, A. Vietnam veterans rap groups: Themes of post-war life. *Journal of Social Issues* 31(4):111-124, 1975.

Eisenhart, R. W. You can't hack it little girl: A discussion of the covert psychological agenda of modern combat training. *Journal of Social Issues* 31(4):13-23, 1975.

Erikson, E. *Identity, Youth and Crisis*. New York, W. W. Norton, 1968.

Figley, C. R., Psychosocial adjustment among Vietnam veterans: An overview of the research, in *Stress Disorders Among Vietnam Veterans: Theory, Research and Treatment*. Edited by Figley, C. R. New York: Brunner/Mazel, 1978.

Figley, C. R. and Leventman, S., eds. *Strangers at Home: Vietnam Veterans Since the War*. New York: Praeger Publications, 1980.

Figley, C. R., ed. *Stress Disorders Among Vietnam Veterans: Theory, Research and Treatment*. New York: Brunner/Mazel, 1978.

Friedman, M. J. Post-Vietnam syndrome: Recognition and management. *Psychosomatics* 22:931-943, 1981.

Frye, J. S. and Stockton, R. A. Discriminant analysis of post-traumatic stress disorder among a group of Vietnam veterans. *American Journal of Psychiatry* 139(1):52-55, January 1982.

Futterman, S. and Pumpian-Mindlin, E. Traumatic war neuroses five years later. *American Journal of Psychiatry* 108:401-408, 1951.

Gelb, L. H. and Betts, R. K. *The Irony of Vietnam: The System Worked*. Washington, D.C.: Brookings Institution, 1971.

Glass, A. J. Psychotherapy in the combat zone. *American Journal of Psychiatry* 110:725-731, 1954.

Glass, A. J. Introduction, in *The Psychology and Physiology of Stress*. Edited by Bourne, P. G. New York: Academic Press, 1969.

Goodwin, J. The etiology of combat-related post-traumatic stress disorders, in *Post-Traumatic Stress Disorders of the Vietnam Veteran*. Edited by Williams, T. Cincinnati, Ohio: Disabled American Veterans, 1980.

Green, B. L., Wilson, J. P. and Lindy, J. D. A conceptual framework for post-traumatic stress syndrome among survivors groups, in *Trauma and Its Wake* (in press). Edited by Figley, C. R.

Green, B. L. Assessing levels of psychological impairment following disaster: Consideration of actual and methodological dimensions. *Journal of Nervous and Mental Disease* 170:544-552, 1982.

Grinker, R. R. and Spiegel, J. P. *Men Under Stress*. Philadelphia: Blakiston, 1945.

Haley, S. A. When the patient reports atrocities. *Archives of General Psychiatry* 30:191-196, 1974.

Helzer, J. E. et. al. Depression in Vietnam veterans and civilian controls. *American Journal of Psychiatry* 136:526-529, 1979.

Hendin, H. et. al. Meanings of combat and the development of post-traumatic stress disorder. *American Journal of Psychiatry* 138:1490-1493, 1981.

Horowitz, M. J. and Solomon, G. F. Delayed stress response syndromes in Vietnam veterans, in *Stress Disorders Among Vietnam Veterans: Theory, Research and Treatment*. Edited by Figley, C. R. New York: Brunner/Mazel, 1978.

Howard, S. the Vietnam warrior: His experiences and implications for psychotherapy. *American Journal of Psychotherapy* 30(1):121-135, 1976.

Jones, F. D. and Johnson, A. W. Medical psychiatric treatment policy and practice in Vietnam. *Journal of Social Issues* 31(4):49-65, 1975.

Kormos, H. R. The nature of combat stress, in *Stress Disorders Among Vietnam Veterans: Theory, Treatment and Research*. Edited by Figley, C. R. New York: Brunner/Mazel, 1978.

Lacoursiere, R. B., Godfrey, K. E. and Ruby, L. M. Traumatic neurosis in the etiology of alcoholism: Vietnam combat and other trauma. *American Journal of Psychiatry* 137:966-968, 1980.

Langley, M. K. Post-traumatic stress disorders among Vietnam combat veterans. *Social Casework* 63:593-598, 1982.

Laufer, R. S. et. al. *Legacies of Vietnam*, Volume 3: Post-war Trauma: Social and Psychological Problems of Vietnam Veterans. Washington, D.C.: Government Printing Office, 1981.

Leventman, S. and Camacho, P. The "gook" syndrome. The Vietnam war as a racial encounter, in *Strangers At Home: Vietnam Veterans Since the War*. Edited by Figley, C. R. Leventman, S. New York: Praeger Publications, 1980.

Lifton, R. J. *Home From the War: Vietnam Veterans—Neither Victims Nor Executioners.* New York: Simon & Schuster, 1973.

Lifton, R. J. *The Broken Connection.* New York: Simon & Schuster, 1980.

Lifton, R. J. and Olson, E. The human meaning of total disaster: The Buffalo Creek Disaster. *Psychiatry* 39:1-18, 1967.

Lifton, R. J. *The Life of The Self.* New York: Simon & Schuster, 1976.

Lindy, J. D. and Titchener, J. Acts of God and man: Long-term character change in survivors of disasters and the law, in *Behavioral Sciences and The Law.* New York: Van Nostrand Reinhold, 1983.

Lindy, J. D., Grace, M. C. and Green, B. L. Survivors: Outreach to a reluctant population. *American Journal of Orthopsychiatry* 51:468-478, 1981.

Lipkin, J. O. et. al. Vietnam veterans and post-traumatic stress disorder. *Hospital and Community Psychiatry* 33:908-912, 1982.

Mantell, D. M. and Pilisuk, M., eds. *Journal of Social Issues: Soldiers In and After Vietnam* 31(4), 1975.

Moskos, C. C. The American combat soldier in Vietnam. *Journal of Social Issues* 31(4):25-37, 1975.

Nace, E. P. et. al. Depression in veterans two years after Vietnam. *American Journal of Psychiatry* 134:167-170, 1977.

Perlman, M. S. Basic problems of military psychiatry: Delayed reaction in Vietnam veterans. *International Journal Offender Therapy and Comparative Criminology,* 19:129-138, 1975.

President's Commission on Mental Health. Report of the special working group: mental health problems of Vietnam era veterans. Washington, D.C., February 15, 1978.

Renner, J. A. Jr. The changing patterns of psychiatric problems in Vietnam. *Comprehensive Psychiatry* 14:169-181, 1973.

Schnaier, J. Female Vietnam veterans and post-traumatic stress disorders: Assessement and implications at National Conference on Post Vietnam Stress Syndrome, Human Resource Initiatives. Dayton, Ohio: 1982.

Shatan, C. F. Stress disorders among Vietnam veterans: The emotional content of combat continues, in *Stress Disorders Among Vietnam Veterans: Theory, Research and Treatment.* Edited by Figley, C. R. New York: Brunner/Mazel, 1978.

Shatan, C. F. The grief of soldiers: Vietnam combat veterans self-help movement. *American Journal of Orthopsychiatry* 43:640-653, 1973.

Strayer, R. and Ellenhorn, L. Vietnam veterans: A study exploring adjustment patterns and attitudes. *Journal of Social Issues* 31(4):81-93, 1975.

Tiffany, W. J. and Allerton, W. S. Army psychiatry in the mid-60s. *American Journal of Psychiatry* 123:810-821, 1967.

Van Putten, T. and Emory, W. H. Traumatic neuroses in Vietnam returnees. *Archives of General Psychiatry* 29:695-698, 1973.

Walker, J. I. Vietnam combat veterans with legal difficulties: A psychiatric problem? *American Journal of Psychiatry* 138:1384-1385, 1981.

Williams, T., ed. *Post-traumatic Stress Disorders of the Vietnam Veteran.* Cincinnati, Ohio: Disabled American Veterans, 1980.

Williams, T. Vietnam veterans. Paper presented at University of Denver, School of Professional Psychology, Denver, Colorado: April 1979.

Wilson, J. P. Conflict, stress and growth: The effects of the Vietnam War on Psychosocial development among Vietnam veterans, in *Strangers At Home: Vietnam Veterans Since the War.* Edited by Figley, C. R., Leventman, S. New York: Praeger Press, 1980.

Wilson, J. P. *Identity, Ideology and Crisis: The Vietnam Veteran in Transition,* Volume II. Washington, D.C.: Disabled American Veterans, 1979.

Wilson, J. P. and Krauss, G. E. Predicting post-traumatic stress syndromes among Vietnam veterans. Cleveland, Ohio: Cleveland State University, 1978.

Wilson, J. P. Towards an understanding of Post-traumatic disorder among Vietnam veterans. Testimony before U.S. Senate Subcommittee on Veterans' Affairs, Washington, D.C. May 21, 1980.

Yalom, I. D. *Existential Psychotherapy.* New York: Basic Books, 1980.

General Books

Amter, Joseph A. *Vietnam Verdict: A Citizen's History.* New York: Continuum, 1982.

Barry, Jan, ed. *Peace Is Our Profession: Poems and Passages of War Protest.* Montclair, N.J.: East River Anthology, 1981.

Caputo, Philip. *A Rumor of War.* New York: Ballentine, 1978.

Del Veccio, John M. *The Thirteenth Valley.* New York: Bantam, 1982.

Egendorf, Arthur. What and Whom there is to forgive, in M. Polner, ed., *When Can I Come Home: Essays on Amnesty.* New York: Doubleday Anchor, 1971.

Emerson, Gloria. *Winners and Losers.* New York: Random House, 1977.

Fitzgerald, Frances. *Fire In The Lake, The Vietnamese and the Americans in Vietnam.* New York: Random House, 1973.

Glasser, Ronald. *Three Hundred and Sixty-five Days.* New York: Braziller, 1971.

Goldman, Peter L. et. al. *Charlie Company: What Vietnam Did To Us.* New York: Morrow, 1983.

Halberstam, David. *The Best and the Brightest.* New York: Fawcett, 1973.

Herr, Michael. *Dispatches.* New York: Alfred A. Knopf, 1968.

Horne, A. D., ed. *The Wounded Generation: America After Vietnam.* Englewood Cliffs, N.J., 1981.

Karnow, Stanley. *Vietnam: A History.* New York: Viking Press, 1983.

Keylin, A., and Boiangiu, S., eds. *Front Page Vietnam: As Reported by the New York:* Arno Press, 1979.

Klein, Robert. *Wounded Men, Broken Promises.* New York: Macmillan, 1981.

Kovic, Ron. *Born On the Fourth of July.* New York: McGraw Hill, 1976.

O'Brien, Tim. *Going After Cacciato.* New York: Dell, 1979.

O'Brien. *If I Die in a Combat Zone.* New York: Dellacort, 1969.

Rottman, Larry, ed. *Winning Hearts and Minds: War Poems by Vietnam Veterans.* Montclair, N.J.: East River Anthology, 1972.

Santoli, Al. *Everything We Had: An Oral History of the Vietnam War as Told by Thirty-three American Soldiers Who Fought It.* New York: Random House, 1981.

Starr, Paul, ed. *The Discarded Army: Veterans After Vietnam.* New York: Charterhouse, 1973.

Van Devanter, Lynda. *Home Before Morning: The Story of an Army Nurse in Vietnam.* New York: Beaufort, 1983.

Webb, James, Jr.: *Fields of Fire.* New York: Bantam, 1979.

General Articles

Broyles, William J. Remembering a war we want to forget. *Newsweek,* November 22, 1982, p. 82.

Bryan, C.D.B. The veterans ordeal (agent Orange). *New Republic,* June 27, 1983, pp. 25-33.

Buckley, Christopher. Viet guilt: Were the real prisoners of war the young Americans who never left home. *Esquire,* September 1983, p. 68.

Butterfield, Fox. The new Vietnam scholarship. *New York Times Magazine,* February 13, 1983, pp. 26-35.

Caputo, Philip. The unreturning army. *Playboy,* January 1982, p. 106.

Corson, William. Advice and dissent: America's treatment of Vietnam vets. *Time,* July 13, 1981, p. 23.

Corson, William. The Vietnam veterans adviser: Agent Orange. *Penthouse,* January 1982, p. 118.

Egendorf, Arthur. The ones who came back. *New York Times.* September 1972.

Egendorf, Arthur. Vietnam goes on. *New York Times,* May 26, 1981.

Egendorf, Arthur. You don't have to be crazy to be a vet. *Penthouse,* April 1974.

Goldman, Peter. What Vietnam did to us. *Newsweek,* December 14, 1981, pp. 46-52.

Hay, John. The ghosts of poisons past (agent Orange). *McLeans,* February 2, 1981, p. 29.

Herr, Michael. Sending the war home. *Esquire,* June 1983, p. 265.

Keerdoja, E. A Vietnam vets toughest battle. *Newsweek,* July 18, 1983, p. 9.

Keerdoja, E. Kovic: Some of the wounds have healed. *Newsweek,* May 9, 1983, p. 13.

Kidder, Tracy. Soldiers of misfortune. *Atlantic,* March 1978, pp. 41-52.

Life. Tracking agent Orange: Vietnam veterans battle insidious foe. December 1981, p. 65.

Lifton, Robert J. The consequence of war: The gook syndrome and numbered warfare. *Saturday Review,* November 18, 1972, pp. 66-72.

Lindley, Forrest Jr. The history of Vietnam veterans. *The Stars & Stripes,* November 11, 1982.

Marin, Peter. Coming to terms with Vietnam. *Harpers,* December 1980, pp. 41-56.

Marin, Peter. Living in moral pain. *Psychology Today,* November 1981, pp. 68-9.

Marin, Peter. What the Vietnam vets can teach us. *The Nation,* November 27, 1982, p. 545+.

Morganthau, Tom. The troubled Vietnam vet. *Newsweek,* March 30, 1981, pp. 24+.

Morrow, Lance. The forgotten warriors. *Time,* July 13, 1981, pp. 18-25.

MS. A delayed reaction. Vietnam casualties at home. September 1980, p. 39.

MS. The other Vietnam vets (women). June 1982, p. 23.

Muller, Robert. Wounds that will not heal. *Time,* July 13, 1981, p. 22.

New York Times. Survey probes causes and manifestations of post-Vietnam syndrome (PVS) suffered by significant number of returning Vietnam veterans. August 21, 1972, p. 1:2.

Norman, Michael, A wound that will not heal. *New York Times Magazine,* November 11, 1979, pp. 134-41+.

O'Brien, Tim. The violent vet. *Esquire,* December 1979, pp. 96-7.

Science News. Aftermath for Vietnam combat veterans. April 11, 1981, p. 236.

Science News. VA's agent Orange exams criticized. November 6, 1982, p. 301.

Stein, Jeffrey. The forgotten vets. *The Progressive,* June 1980, pp. 14-15.

Time. Dividend from Vietnam. October 10, 1969, pp. 60-61.

Time. The War Came Home. April 6, 1981, p. 17.